Beyond All This

Thirty Years with the Mountain People of Haiti

Oneta Cole

Mildred Anderson

Light Messages

Published 2010, by Light Messages
www.lightmessages.com
Durham, NC 27713 USA
SAN: 920-9298

Paperback ISBN: 978-0-98007-563-2
Ebook ISBN: 978-1-61153-036-0

Contents

Acknowledgments

F riends who for years have received Granny Holdeman's letters have also kept them. The feeling that here was something so extraordinary that it would bear rehearsing had stirred more than sentiment, for many of these people had never seen Granny more than once in their lives. Most of them had given something to the little mission in the mountains of Haiti with no clear idea of where it was in the Caribbean.

When Granny's daughter, Eleanor Turnbull, sent out a plea for help in compiling data for Granny's story, literally scores of replies included Granny's chronicling of her own day-to-day dispensary stress and distress, teaching new converts, the mission children and her own three little grandsons, gardening and cooking. Most of these letters were written on the back and along the margins of mission newsletters or on all the space she could find on a greeting card. Sensitive to this land's bondage, to its superstition and fear, she described lengthy Voodoo rites, misadventures with fire and firewater, spells and saturnalia. She suffered with these people the catastrophic disasters of three hurricanes, with flood, drought, starvation and disease in their wake. Yet, in good times and bad, she rejoiced that the work grew. There was some joy and celebration for each day. She thanked God for all things great and small, her red hibiscus, fine melons, new peas and potatoes, the ever welcome guests who came to the mission.

From these letters sent by the Greenfields, the Northcrosses, the Searses, the Bells, the Radkes, the Walkers, the Davises, the Pilses, the Peekses, the Cornwells, the Pintzes, the Williamses, Joyce Garner and dozens more, much has been taken.

Eleanor's diary accounts of back-country treks, told with humor and pathos, sensitivity and éclat—oh, well, if the pig and goat can thrive on it, so can we—added much more.

Sandy and Wally, are both adept with words. With David, they all grew up on the island and offered germane insight into the Haitian culture.

Wallace, cogent and understanding as perhaps no other foreigner has understood these people with whom he is patiently investing his life to help them save themselves, gave enormous inspiration and aid.

No one in this remarkable family could have stayed with it had there not been the "call", the personal dedication, the constant reliance on Him whose grace is sufficient, and the vision to see this island again become the paradise Columbus discovered and described.

And there's Granny who gave precious hours on tape, yet was more eager to suggest trips to include the island's charm and loveliness, or to recall those other years when a destiny intertwined the lives of our north Mississippi families.

For all the hours of talk and demonstration and excursion there in Haiti, and for the invaluable assistance of Beverly Linsley in the Grand Rapids office, all of which made this story possible, the acknowledgment of indebtedness is deep-felt.

It is unlikely that as one travels, one will encounter extremes of culture and ignorance, grace and need, exhilaration and despair, along with the beauty, the selflessness and love translated that one finds in Granny's Haiti.

If you never go there, this little book was written with you in mind.

This Story

*She did not shiver although the
evening was cold. A little bit hunched,
her slight frame disaffirming any
frailty, she stood pointing to the
southeastern sky where Venus and
Jupiter were brightly identifiable
above a brilliant streak that dipped
into the sea. The group around
her was listening intently as she
explained that it was a comet. To
most of them, all young Haitian men,
she was their only source of such
learning. She was saying in melodic
Creole that it may be many miles
across, the tail composed of thin
gases and particles of dust flowing
millions of miles away from the sun;
also that there are many comets, few
visible without a telescope. Back in
1910, when she was near their age,
she saw the most famous one of all,
Haley's Comet, not so large as this
one, but due to return in 1986.*

Granny was born in 1888. Some call her the Mary Slessor of Haiti; others think of her as the Grandma Moses of missions.

Granny went to Haiti in 1947 to become a missionary to the mountain people. Less than two months after reaching the island, her promise of private financial backing abruptly dried up. Over age to expect denominational tenure on the mission field, she nonetheless determined to stay in the work she had commenced. "The Lord brought me down here; He will take care of me." Some days seeing as many as 300 patients in her dispensary work, she learned to speak Creole and patiently set about introducing these superstitious Voodoo worshipers to the Christian way of life.

Her first year on the island, Granny spent three dollars on clothes for herself. There were other years she probably spent no more. When the young head of the mission, Wallace Turnbull, became her son-in-law in the year following Eleanor's visit down to scrutinize her mother's situation, the three became the mission staff. Although the mission was sponsored by Conservative Baptists (Grand Rapids, Michigan), it was, with the help of Stateside friends, for the most part self-sustaining. Presently the mission ministers to 55,000 converts, over 140 churches, while operating the 150bed hospital and TB wards, 162 schools with over 20,000 students, Family Care Center, Mountain Maid outlet shop and tearoom, experimental farms and gardens, guest houses and all else that comprise the mission compound.

A few years ago, in an effort to provide learning opportunity for a greater number of children in the rural mountain areas of Haiti, Granny began paying the mission children who had already learned to read and write to teach others. This adaptation of Laubach's one-child-teach-another experiment spread with such ardor, Granny's resources quickly vanished. Had it not been for a matching eagerness back in the States of friends who sent small amounts, some large, Haiti's unprecedented surge to learn would not be attracting the far spread attention it is or climaxing Granny's story so dramatically.

Because of Granny's one-child-teach-another plan throughout the rural island, thousands of school children crowd mission schools in exciting social revolution.

Preface

*Dear Lord, if only we could be a
hundred, yea, a thousand!*

Year after year, Bertha Holdeman had urged me to visit
Haiti. Finally I went, after giving my air mail letter two
weeks to reach its destination. To lessen the worry for her
daughter Eleanor and her, the Lord obligingly got the word of my
arrival to them an hour before my plane circled the green patchwork
slopes about Port-au-Prince, then skimmed the blue, blue sea again
before leveling off and touching down on the runway of François
Duvalier Airport, mellow white in the late afternoon sun. We were
played into the station by Papa Doc's lively band.

A smiling porter bowed me through customs, "Madame
Wallace votre ami? Ah-h-h, thees way!" Through the airport, gay
with murals painted by Haiti's famed primitive artists, and three
more smiling porters hustled my two bags into a station wagon,
from which my friend for most of my life and her daughter Eleanor
flung themselves in greeting. Time was to ride at anchor in the
days ahead.

Distance vanished in the haze of heat and the surge of vehicles
ricocheting along the highway. Camions, the Haitian bus, gaily
painted, snorting with their double deck burden of humanity,
turkeys and chickens and baskets of produce; donkeys trotting
under a double burden too, if not a woman and a bundle, paired
bundles strapped to their backs; publiques, with identifying red
banners, the Haitian taxis; trucks and open cars, all weaving in
and out, jockeying for space in a stream of French-built Renaults
and Peugeots, those who had them cutting staccato didos on their
horns. This perpetual hurry converged on the city in a maelstrom.
Only the main street of Port-au-Prince grudgingly conceded to
order. This street has traffic lights. At the telephone exchange
(telephone service has not been built to the mission) Wallace joined
us and took the wheel. The human current overflowed the narrow

sidewalk and eddied into the streets, women in colorful cottons, girls in miniskirts, men mostly in work clothes, with a sprinkling in business suits.

Nimble columns of pedestrian traffic lined both sides of the mountain road leaving the city and moved with such swiftness they dragged the city up with them; then they began thinning to coveys of foot travelers. Suddenly night fell, and their dark hurrying forms merged with the shadows of the flamboyant trees and poinsettias bordering the roadside.

Halfway up, Petionville, favorite suburb of aristocrat Haitians, diplomats and foreign residents, for a sweeping view of the capital and the Bay of Gonâve beyond, spread upward with luxurious homes and deluxe hotels and inns.

Another 3,000 feet up we turned into the mission compound. Against the low stone wall entrance a group of shadowy figures waited. Lights were on in the new Mountain Maid tearoom, the Christmas star glowed above the church façade, and workers still carried sand and concrete to the site of the new Family Care Center. Across the way other groups waited on the hospital gallery. Voices and cooking smells wafted up from the convalescent wards.

Down past a guest house a chimney and roof were etched against the evening sky, the rest of the stone house so caressed by bougainvillea, hibiscus, ten foot begonias, oleanders and poinsettias, it was hardly there. "Granny's house," said Eleanor. The tropical flowerage stretched with us down the driveway to the end and the beginning of the mission compound-Wallace's and Eleanor's house. This inviting sprawling structure with vine covered atrium, held somewhere within it the first three rooms Wallace built in 1947, the home that Bertha made until her daughter came the next year to join Wallace in a lifetime venture of helping this land, tasting its troubles, and savoring fervent hopes for it.

Night followed night of after dinner conversation, day after day of excursions over the island. Then, one night, Eleanor brought in the letters. Neighbors and friends who remembered Bertha in Tennessee, in the hill country of north Mississippi, friends from

Denver to Grand Rapids and back to Miami and Haiti, all offered their recollections and reminiscences of this remarkable woman for her life story. Only those who had known her longest called her Bertha Holdeman. She was Granny to everybody else.

The text and tempo of my visit altered, sleep did not come readily. The chorus of night sounds outside my window intoned with a special meaning. Granny deserved a luminous focus with a blazing torch, no feeble candle held aloft. In the spirit and dedication of this lone woman who had faced formidable and dreadful odds to bring light to a dark land and to change a vast hopelessness to hope there burned a quenchless message. I demurred. Maybe if I prayed for humility and the turning of a phrase... I would try.

Finally the nearer insect voices helped me to drift into sleep.

Awake before the usual activities of the compound began, I got up and stole across the living room to watch the morning light feel its way over the distant mountains and, like a zephyr, magically clear the mist-filled valley. The day's beginning in Haiti is a splendorous experience. The sky's complexion changes from the purple darkness of Granny's pansies to the lavender-pink of her bougainvillea; then in a vast extravagance of shading yields to amber and green before this miracle of a tropical dawn dissolves in pure turquoise.

Soon after breakfast, under the clump of pines above the vegetable garden, Granny and I began our sessions—well away from the stir of the house and laundry and hospital cooking.

"These pines were a handful of seedlings Mrs. Paul of Huntingdon, Indiana, gave in 1967, she observed. "Oh, and there will be strawberries for dessert tonight," surveying the scattered red orbs along the rows below. "We have them from November to May."

The sun had driven away the morning chill and glinted warmly through the pines, touching up Granny's reddish gold braid that still reached full circle... As if in reverie, she began:

First a committee came down to look over the mission potential. The three room house was the only thing on the site that resembled permanence, and it still had a dirt floor. A thatched roof of vetiver grass sheltered a few poles from the hot sun. These poles were benches for the encouraging number of curious mountain people who came to hear the Good News. The committee took a look at Granny's public clinic under the avocado trees—a hand hewn chair and a two foot square box of specifics for disorders tropical. This dispensary was bringing enough comfort and relief to those who risked Granny and her Jamaican interpreter, by this time three hundred and more daily brought their boils and ulcers, their burns and rashes, their fevers and parasites, their bad teeth and dysentery, and went away helped.

"I'm going to stay whether you include support for me or not," announced this fifty nine year old woman who thirty-six years before had booked passage to Africa but was refused a visa because during World War I anyone of German extraction was suspect.

Thirty odd years have woven strong ties that have bound her spirit to this sad and lovely island, this fascinating and mysterious land, where great beauty and squalor exist side by side. Strongest are the bonds of sympathy and affection which undeniably unite her heart and the hearts of fifty thousand rural Haitians whose lives she can now see beginning to change wondrously.

Since they won their freedom nearly two hundred years ago, they have been content to go on living the ways of their African ancestors. In the daytime the men and boys work at whatever they can find to make a few pennies. The women are in their gardens, save on market days. They dig a daily supply of manioc (cassava from which comes our tapioca) or other roots, hike to the spring where they wash and bathe, fill their gourds, and gather enough bits of firewood to make the evening fire. All the day they may carry their babies slung from their shoulders. In the evening there is much talk and laughter and dancing. The night sparkles with these small fires under their cooking pots. The men sprawl patiently after the day's labor and the children play naked in the cluttered dooryards. The pots boil with roots and greens and a little oil, or with mush and red beans, the one big meal of the day.

Once the whole island was rich and verdant. Pine, mahogany, oak and coffee canopied all the mountain slopes. Careless timbering and charcoal making have, over the years, exposed them so severely to erosion that the mountain sides have lost their capacity to soak up even a normal rain. The water rushes downward, gouging the slopes and moving precious topsoil with it. By landslide and erosion, tons of soil from the mountains have reached the bay, to bed the modern new development of Port-au-Prince and her new airport.

"We believe the mission's terracing program is the answer to cumulative erosion," continued Granny. "Only after the tragedy of three recent hurricanes have the mountain people, perilously clinging to their own rocky precipice, come to see that they must abandon primitive practices to survive. With no place to escape, their sons and daughters are turning away from the old hereditary superstitions and easygoing culture. It is no longer earth moving to get them to change."

The picture is a moving one. "With little public education in Haiti, the desire to learn is so impelling and the forces of change are gathering such momentum, we have seen illiteracy drop from 98 percent to 80 percent. Polygamy, which kept the Haitian woman in bondage, is another crumbling part of the old cultural structure. The Christian concept brings dramatic change in their lives. Christian marriages attended by grown offspring are encouragingly now less common."

As I look over these mountainsides and see the lovely green checkered terraces; see the women sitting in their doorways doing needlework and crafts to earn school fees that their children may learn to 'hold the book'; see the streams of eager children on their way to school, I cry, 'Dear Lord, if only we could be a hundred, yea, a thousand! With strength to teach, to demonstrate, to encourage, and never to turn away one eager child or one earnest man seeking the better way; to help them grow more corn and millet up-breed their goats and cows, and lift their burden of fear How well we know the harvest is white.'

Antoine had stood waiting for Granny to pause, "Madame, a pan full," he was smiling. "A lot indeed! Give it to Dieula," she instructed, approving the panful of honey in the comb robbed that morning. The peaked chunks were oozing amber nectar. Granny chuckled, "You should have seen David teaching him to rob the bees!" Her voice had a tolling quality, like the forte parlando of small carillon bells, especially when she laughed, and then it was as if the carillonneur pulled them all at once.

The sun rode high overhead.

Greta Cole

Haiti

H aiti is the middle island between Cuba and Puerto Rico, part of the string of islands called the Greater Antilles.

Hardly as graceful as "the big white swan that glides on a lovely lake," finger play you did as a child, Haiti looks more like a duck's beak that forms when you cup your right hand and then widen the space between your thumb and forefinger. At the base of your thumb is the capitol, Port-au-Prince. The tip of your forefinger is northwest, your stretched thumb is the south and southwest peninsula. Your knuckles are north and the ragged cuff is east and the Dominican border.

Seven league boots would serve well in seeing this mountainous island, but a jeep is next best. If you take off from the second joint of your index finger, your first stop will be Cap Haitien, redolent with history. Settled by the French in 1670, it is near the spot where Columbus left the crew of his Santa Maria which, on Christmas Eve 1492, broke up on a reef off the north shore of the island. (The anchor reposes in the national museum.) Everywhere in Haiti there are people to show the way, change a tire, get you across a river or through a flood. Now that you are in unhurried Cap Haitien, a handful of natives will suddenly become a score who eagerly offer to go with you to Milot, watch your jeep, get you a horse or a donkey to make the grueling journey everybody who comes here makes—the climb to the Citadelle. You give it the day.

The Citadelle, an awesome structure called the eighth wonder of the world, was built by Henri Christophe, to defy Napoleon. Christophe was the first leader of this people, who freed themselves from slavery with no outside help. He conscripted the whole population of north Haiti from 1804 to 1817 to labor on this mountaintop fortress with walls ten feet thick and shaped like the prow of a ship, its ramparts surmounted by 365 cannon. Intended to be a fortress that would forever defy the French, it was an incredible feat of engineering. Thirty thousand men are said to have died quarrying, hauling and handing the stone blocks up a two-mile human chain to the summit of La Ferrière. With vast ammunition and powder rooms, dungeons, and treasure chambers (many still sealed and unexplored), this massive structure was designed to maintain a garrison of sixteen hundred men with provisions for months. It is also said that the contractor, who alone shared with Christophe the secrets of this awesome monument, trod the same path with 200 of the king's soldiers who obediently marched from the 3,000 foot height into the abyss at the command of their king.

At the base of the mountain, at Milot, the ruins of Christophe's palace once rivaled in splendor the finest in Europe. This wondrous complex covered twenty acres. Walls of brick overlaid with stucco rose four stories high, executing a bold, spatial concept with paired colonnades and balconies. Floors of marble and mosaic, polished mahogany walls, tapestries from the world's most famous looms, bathrooms, air conditioning with cold mountain streams flowing through conduits underneath the floor (and emerging in beautiful fountains)—all this, and royal stables which once housed Christophe's English carriage (costing 700 English pounds), paralleled France's best. (The end came for the monarch Christophe when he suffered a stroke and his army and courtiers deserted. He is said to have shot himself with a silver bullet, and the queen and one faithful retainer carried his huge body on a mule up the precipitous trail and dumped it in a vat of quicklime. A plaque on the ramparts declares the date of his death—1820).

Toping La Ferrièr in massive silence, this fortress is called the Citadelle and eighth wonder of the world.

Feeling yourself also frozen in time, and clinging to your horse like a salamander, you leave this massively silent cloud tipped eminence to make the steep descent to sea level again.

Your next stop is Port-de-Paix, oldest city on the island where the dove haunted ruins of an old church (dating from 1540) enshrine the island's oldest edifice. Offshore is the small island of Tortuga that gave refuge to adventurers and pirates in the 1500's (Spanish galleons laden with gold and silver from the Aztec and Inca empires were prizes coveted by French and British adventurers of the sea).

Round the tip of the island, touch Gonaïves, made famous by revolutionary leader Dessalines who drove the French from the island in 1803. Even though your narrow road roughens and your jeep hovers on the verge of a chasm, stay with it until you reach St. Marc, passing the cotton, rice, and sugarcane fields; then on to Duvalierville and Port-au-Prince, which you will visit many times.

It is standard procedure to check in at a police post. Roads are hazardous, river crossings more so, and cars have been known to plummet down a mountainside where the only guard rails are space. The native will recognize a tree branch stuck in a hole for warning; you may have plunged into a washout cleft before you make the connection. The police will know where to look for you if you fail to return, or, if you are suspect, what you are up to.

Travel inside your thumb 200 miles along the coast line, cross three rivers and reach Jérémie by the cliff road which the Marines built while Haiti was a ward of the U.S. after the massacre and murder of General Guillame Sam in 1915. This quaint southern tip town of coffee, cocoa and logwood, stucco houses painted pink and green, was the birthplace of Alexander Dumas, French novelist and dramatist. Here also lived Émile Roumère, Creole poet. Farther along the southern coast line you will turn inland to visit the island's greatest waterfall, Saut-Mathurine. If you drop down to Les Cayes, you will see the old forts, hear how the young republic in 1815 gave men, ships, arms and provisions to Simon Bolivar in his struggle to free Columbia, Peru and Bolivia from the rule of Spain. Bolivar's gift of a gold sword to President Pétion also hangs in the national museum.

On past the knuckle of your thumb to Jacmel and Belle Anse, formerly Sale Trou (Dirty Hole), are the last points on your thousand mile trek. These remote villages on the windward side of the island are at the end of a river road. Your jeep fords the stream again and again, even follows it from time to time, until it brings you over an ancient bridge that curtsies to Jacmel, a town so quaintly charming you find yourself back in plantation days. You wander past gingerbread houses with wrought iron balcony rails, stone walls and sheltered garden terraces, lush tropical vegetation, moss and orchids and butterflies. You listen to laborers among the banana and cocoa groves singing haunting chanties. Narrow winding streets lead to the waterfront that discloses almost unexplored reaches of seashore along the serene, blue Caribbean. It is easy to feel here the peace and beauty the famous painter Préfèt Dufaut was able to put on his canvases.

You can return to Port-au-Prince, but take a few side trips. Visit the breadbasket of the island, the Artibonite Valley where children romp in the streams while the women pound their family wash with wooden paddles. Cross the hot, dry region studded with ash-green cacti to Des Chapelles and the Mellons, peerless, heart expanding Albert Schweitzer Hospital in the lowlands. Your jeep will strain many times over the rugged back country territory, but you will find real adventure exploring the Pre-Columbian grottoes (with pictographs by the Arawak Indians), waterfalls and plantations of the north and east.

As you make your way back to the city, houses become picturesque and spacious. They seem to grow out of the mountainsides, their balconies and parabolas designed to funnel the breezes. The air grows cooler as you continue to climb, until, 4,000 feet up, you pause at a new roadside restaurant. From its balcony you watch the lights of the city come on and circle a glimmering necklace around Gonâve Bay, then you make the climb to the mission.

Turnbull

*In all his travels, it seemed to John
Turnbull that the needs of this
area were the most desperate.*

I n 1916, John Turnbull, a young missionary and linguist,
embarked for India, where, his term scarcely begun, he was
stricken with typhoid, then malaria, and was sent into the
hills to recover. At Ooty, he met a fervent young Presbyterian
missionary, Maude Smith, whom he soon persuaded to make their
commitment one, and, married, the couple served out their term at
Ahmedabad. Here one son was born, and the second, Wallace, was
conceived before the Turnbulls started home on their first furlough.
Before leaving India, the Turnbulls resolved to go to Agra to see
the Taj Mahal. At the reflecting pool, John stopped and gathered
a handful of lotus pods which he carried in his pocket until the
little family reached Los Angeles where John's father lived, and
where Maude's second son was born in a Hollywood hospital.
That summer day, walking beside the newly formed Echo Lake,
largest artificial lake in the county, John tossed the lotus pods into
the water. Years later, the splendor of the lotus blossoms on the
surface became a tourist attraction. (Learning, of this story, the
superintendent of parks wrote Wallace in Haiti to tell him that
the Lotus Festival was set for July 10, Wallace's birthday, and he
enclosed a festival brochure with exotic pictures of the show at its
peak.)

John and Maude were next sent to the Middle East, where John
became the first man to cross the Arabian Desert in an automobile,
and thereafter to become a life member of the Royal Geographic
Society.

Tragedy soon struck a series of blows in the life of the young missionary traveler. His young wife Maude died following the birth of her third son. Wallace, barely two years old, was taken back to the States to Nyack, New York, where his Uncle Walter was head of the Christian and Missionary Alliance and his Aunt Cora became his beloved foster mother. But Aunt Cora was taken from him in death before he was three, and two years later his uncle died in an automobile accident.

John Turnbull married again, the depression years came on, and John's work as deputation secretary, evangelist and minister took the little family through many moves, from North Carolina to Oregon. When he was asked to make a worldwide tour of C.M.A. missions, son Wallace was placed in a boarding school in a rural South Carolina community where mainly, in the fullness of time, a vegetarian diet, hard work, and rigid religious training were calculated to hollow most of the youngsters for the mission field. Wallace's college years were spent at Marion College, in Marion, Indiana.

On the missions tour, Dr. Turnbull surveyed the little island of Haiti. Dr. Maurice Armand, brother-in-law to President Lescot, at the president's request, drove Dr. Turnbull up the mountain to a place called Fermathe, which the president implied might be a mission site. At that time, infant mortality for the area was 75 percent. Polygamy, belief in witchcraft, zombies and evil spirits prevailed, roads were mud or dust, and illiteracy was 98 percent.

And so it was, in October 1946, John Turnbull, his trained nurse wife Rhoda, and the twenty one year old Wallace, eager to invest his life in an underdeveloped hinterland, arrived at the wharf in Port-au-Prince by boat. Their chattels comprised a quantity of secondhand tin roofing, a kerosene stove, two mattresses, some carpenter's tools, two kegs of nails, and some lanterns. Port-au-Prince, an unregenerate cohesion of 125,000 restless souls, their coffee drying in the streets, was mindful of an occasional passing sleek government or merchant's car but not at all of the world beyond its coast line.

The Turnbulls made their way twenty miles up the mountain to Fermathe. With $1,800 they bought three acres of unsavory Voodoo stigma, rented a small house across the road, and with an interpreter began making contacts with the people. Rhoda started giving first aid and Wallace set about planning to improve the property.

John and Rhoda soon left the new field to young Wallace, thus opening the way for their friend, Bertha Holdeman, to take up the work in the spring of 1947. Eleanor, her daughter, came down at Christmas to look over her mother's circumstances, Cupid took a hand, and Wallace and Eleanor were wed in August, 1948. Three sons, Wally, Walter (Sandy), and David, came to bless this union and to change Bertha's name to Granny.

Granny

When one studies Granny's face, pared down by ninety years, one finds an intaglio of plain, deep cut unfalseness. The homeliest of faces, it is a countenance immensely telling, with eyes that see with compassion, yet around which plays a smile that may abruptly overrun her whole face, and, full tilt, break into rippling laughter. The mood may grow quickly serious, sensitive, and strong. One would suspect that in all her life, there had been little that was easy. "Like Topsy, I grew up and the frost bit me off," she quipped.

I f Granny's home were a hut in a wasteland, it would charm visitors. "I feel the day is wasted if I haven't planted something or preserved something," she confessed, completing a few chores. She took from the oven the sweet potato pudding she would send over to Eleanor's kitchen for the evening meal. She filled a can and watered the plants near the windows in her L-shaped living room—a room ineluctably Haitian. But a few pieces from Missouri and Mississippi, the fireplace, the books, and the plants imbued the room with a modest middle American pulse and contentment.

Josèf was at the screen door, silhouetted against the blossoms on the retaining wall. Granny had anticipated his appearance.

"These are for the tearoom," she said in Creole, handing him a tin of chocolates and a batch of fresh peanut brittle. "And these for the road stand," loading him with two jars of pickles and some pots of flowers.

"Above and below us are summer places," Granny explained.

"Those from the city buy flowering plants at the mission road stand. I never have enough fuchsias." She went for a can of water to anoint the plants she had set out the day before underneath the bougainvillea and sweet peas that drenched the wall and little porch with bloom. Beyond the kitchen door other things wanted a drink too.

"This celery brings a dollar a stalk. And one of the resort hotels offered to contract for daily delivery of calla lilies," she confided. The callas were beginning to open. Calendulas, amaryllis, blue clustering lily of the Nile, candy tuft—all bloomed in riotous blending down the terraced backyard, and invaded the vegetable and strawberry rows bordering the lily pond.

Granny interrupted herself to greet an upstanding young man who had appeared, smiling broadly. He stooped for her embrace.

"This is Reynaud, and he's returning to school tomorrow." The two exchanged a few words before he told her goodbye.

When he had gone, Granny began his story.

Catule had come sadly despairing that he and Marie were unable to raise a child. Six little graves and not one child living. They were sure it was the witch doctor's curse. Pregnant again Marie had sent Catule to Granny. Would she take this baby? She and her husband had become fervent Christians and when the child was born the father did enough work around the mission compound to enable the little family to live nearby and Granny did watch closely over the baby. As he grew she taught him to read both Creole and English so that when he was only about nine years old he went about the mountains with his lay evangelist father to read the Scriptures for him. He did well in school. Now a student in the French school in Port-au-Prince he had studied both Latin and Greek and would soon be qualified to teach. Granny's approval was apparent. Reynaud would be a Christian teacher.

"There's very little Christian literature in Creole. A little more in French. Of the many young people who crowd my English class not a few are stirred with ambition to leave Haiti, to find the better life. But I tell them the better life will be here when they can read Christian literature in English and can take up the challenge to help their own people," Granny was convinced.

She left the watering of vegetables and strawberries to two small boys (ubiquitous is the word for Haitians; they are everywhere), and we found a place to sit together on a stone ledge. There in the bright winter sunshine, apart from the noises and activity of the mission compound, we talked.

Granny let her mind wander back to the Missouri farm where she grew up in a sturdy but complex German family.

Gottlieb Halstenberg, Granny's father, was sent by his German parents to America early in the 1870's. The Kaiser had lowered the draft age to sixteen, and Gottlieb made the voyage as a stowaway to escape the army. He and his friends settled in central Missouri in the bend of the Missouri River about forty miles east of the promising new state capitol Jefferson City. Gottlieb was soon prospering as a wheat and corn grower, and selling his grain to the riverboats. Even as a young man he was wealthy by that era's reckoning.

By a first marriage Gottlieb became the father of John, Henry, Herman, Maggie, and Mary, the last only six weeks old when her mother died of childbed fever. Gottlieb then married an eighteen year old school teacher, Elizabeth Zeitz, who bore him Lydia, Fred, Willie, Bertha, and Otto. All of these children grew up, along with four orphan Redaker nieces and nephews of Gottlieb's, in a spacious farmhouse where five meals a day marked their plenteous way of life. He died when Bertha was four years old. Elizabeth took unto herself a second husband, whose talents as a provider were obscured by overmuch patronage of the local tavern.

When Bertha started school, she walked the three miles with the other children to the small rural schoolhouse, stayed all day, then came home to help with the chores. She remembered stirring apple butter in a big copper kettle with a long fork-like paddle. She remembered also the two fifty gallon barrels in the cellar. One, the children would fill with cucumbers in brine for pickles. After a time, these would be taken out and lowered in cloth bags into the spring fed well for a day of crisping. The other barrel held sauerkraut for hearty dinners with fresh pork or with knockwurst. And eggs kept well in the cellar. Her mother would go into town with several baskets of fresh eggs, ask no more than six cents a dozen, and would often return home with half of them. There were also great crocks of milk from which the cream would be skimmed and taken up to the kitchen to be churned into butter. Then all the children would sit on the cellar door and eat their fill of the clabber, which is first cousin to yogurt. All the remaining healthful curd they would dump into the pigs trough.

Elizabeth, a woman of rugged frontier stock held the family together with strength and example that matched her precept. She saw to it that each child in this whole lusty brood of sixteen learned first to work then to rest. She taught them to tackle a hard task with vigor and intelligence and never let it go unmastered. And because her children now with Stella and Edna by this second marriage heard her laugh often and could depend on her loving embrace they grew up reverencing the earth's beauty as well as its bounty, because she did. She died when Bertha was eleven.

Bertha missed her mother and wanted to go to heaven where she was. Going to church comforted somewhat but it was three miles to the little German meeting house. Early in the week she would begin entreating one of her brothers to promise to walk with her to church on Sunday. Singing hymns brought her a special happiness. She learned dozens of them by heart.

"The preacher had lost a limb in the war. He would ask the children to come up and pray, then he would ask if we felt better. I didn't know that I did. I tried to read my mother's German Bible but it meant nothing," she was saying.

Soon there was a new stepmother and two babies. One day Bertha was making some starch and a little spattered on one of the little ones. She could not get over the stepfather's stern rebuke. And although the stepfather raised cattle, he continued to dissipate the Halstenberg holdings until even the homestead was mortgaged. However, Bertha and the other children had been saved $2,000 each as they reached legal age.

When Bertha turned eighteen and could claim her small patrimony, she went to St. Louis to find a job. Staying in her older brother's home, she cared for the small son while his mother practiced her music.

Bertha had grown up with the disciplines of menial work. Uncomplaining, she accepted hard work, no matter how hard, as her lot, believing that self respect and that genuine Christian virtue, lowliness of mind, are compatible. How could she balk at the grim and revolting experience of cleaning up after a dysentery patient, or quail at faces and extremities sloughing away with yaws, or wounds infested with maggots? "I was no doubt being conditioned in my early years to understand and later to teach against the sin of pride. The Bible has more to say about this sin than any other. And so insulated in spirit had I grown against the things of the world, when a cousin took me to the theater, I cried and could not enjoy being there."

It was not long after she went to St. Louis that she heard a preacher who convinced her that she really had never known the Lord. Finally during the invitation she sat crying while others went down. An old grey haired man seeing her distress came to her and asked if she wanted to be a Christian. He told her to read John 3:36 with him and then he prayed with her. From that day her life was changed. Not long afterward she heard a missionary from Africa speak then she read his message in a little pamphlet which ended with Isaiah's Here am I; send me. Her heart yearned to go to those who lived in darkness and fear, and she begged the Lord to let her go and try to make a difference in their lives.

First she had to have more education than the country school had provided. She applied for admission to the Missionary Training Institute in Nyack, New York and there she spent four arduous years. Knowing that if she should be sent to a place like Africa she would need all the knowledge of medicine she could acquire, she took every premed course offered, in addition to the nurse training. She thought of the hardships the missionary had described in a land of two seasons, a rainy season and a dry season; of a primitive people who lived in huts, suffered insect borne diseases fevers and dysentery, malignant skin diseases, and malnutrition.

At last she was ready to embark for the mission field. It was 1918. The United States was at war with Germany. With her passport, personal baggage, camping equipment and other supplies that well wishing friends had provided for back country survival in Africa, she arrived at customs in New York. The young man ahead of her passed through without a hitch. When she moved up the officer scanned her credentials. With a suspicious air, he consulted his books, then walked over for a consultation with his superior. Her name was Halstenberg. Her background was German. They decided to deny her a visa.

This crushing disappointment not easily quelled, she went weeping back to Nyack. Dr. A. B. Simpson, founder of the Christian and

Missionary Alliance, came to her room where he found her crying. He knelt beside her chair and prayed in a deep voice. "Thanks be to God who always causeth us to triumph in Christ Jesus. Miss Halstenberg, I'm going! You will be all right. Come to my office at 3:00."

In his office he counseled, "We'll send you to another place and hope that later you can go to Africa."

Sent to Dover, Tennessee, to do home mission work, Granny remembers the few years spent there as a happy chapter in her life. The people belonged to one of two churches, the Methodist or the Christian. It was a labor of love, teaching and visiting and sharing the lives of all the people of this small community.

"It was near Cumberland City," she was still reminiscing, "the hometown of Cordell Hull, then Secretary of State. I knew Cordell's father, an old man who had made a lot of money but who continued to work and live like a poor man. Mr. Hull wore old faded and patched overalls and always a smudged, wilted cap. Once when he was going to Washington to visit Cordie, as he called him, he prepared a bottle of buttermilk and some corn bread for his trip. He left by steamboat on the Cumberland River for Nashville, and from there he traveled by train to the nation's capitol. He was met in Washington by his statesman son, who took him to a department store for a new suit and a new hat. Rather reluctantly he dressed up to please his renowned son and the Washington dignitaries. But when he returned to Cumberland City he was wearing his old overalls and wilted cap and telling his hometown people that he had said to his son, 'Cordie, you needn't be ashamed of this old cap. It's what got you to Washington!,' "

In 1920 Granny left Dover. Before leaving, the people gave her a little farewell fun time. They all came, the whole town, and most of them were on the program. At length, a lawyer rose and said what all of them had attempted: The night was never too dark, nor the weather too cold or stormy for Bertha to come to them when one of them was ill or needed help. It had been her life that had spoken to their hearts. Now life was dearer because her life had touched theirs.

Touched by the appeal of Virginia Holdeman, her former roommate, Bertha had consented to go to Mississippi to nurse Virginia's brother's dying wife. Dr. Holdeman ran a small sanitarium in the then rather remote hill country, several miles from the nearest town or railroad. After the death of Bertha's patient, he persuaded her to remain as assistant in his practice. They were married the following year.

Reminiscences of friends reflect Bertha's new life role, which spanned the next twenty years.

Mary Ethel Butler recalled: One springtime morning, a year or so after Dr. Holdeman married Bertha, I went with my parents, who enjoyed visiting with the Holdemans. We drove up the long tree shaded lane to the rambling fieldstone country house. As Papa reined the horses in the yard, Miss Bertha, as she was called, came briskly from the garden to greet us. Her thick, bright red hair was braided and wound around her head, a few wisps falling about her fair, lightly freckled face. The picture of health, she walked with confidence and poise, heavier than when we last saw her, for she was with child.

On this visit we spent the night. At the evening meal her husband said, "Sweetheart, will you express thanks?" and she said grace for the meal. The next day was Sunday and we went with the Holdemans to Pine Grove Church. Both carried Bibles and taught and prayed. I know now that in Miss Bertha's church teaching, nursing sick neighbors, and busy home life, God was preparing her for an extraordinary work in a difficult field. She had to be tested and tried, work and faint not, serve, love, and suffer, until He called her out in her later years.

From another friend and neighbor, Willard Wallis: With me when my daughter was born, Bertha was always by my side when I needed her. A few years later, when this child was seriously ill, Bertha nursed her four days and nights without rest. And when filling her own pantry and storeroom with the produce of her garden, she shared with the women of the countryside, teaching them nutrition, how to prepare better meals, how to can meats and fruits and corn and beans and tomatoes. Those were the days before we had a county home demonstration agent to bring us improved ways of food preparation. Pellagra plagued the lives of many whose diet consisted mostly of fatback or sow belly and hominy or corn pone... and any whose patronage of a moonshine still further depleted his nutritive needs. They were also the days when cotton quilts and husk filled mattresses did less to exclude the cold than Bertha's wool shorn from the family flock or her down plucked from her own geese.

And, always, as Bertha taught her own children, she gathered in the children of the countryside to tell them precious stories from the Bible.

And from Mildred Anderson: How we missed the Holdemans when they moved to Florida! The years had welded our two families. Our town schools offered more than the rural school attended by Eleanor and Mayo. Eleanor, with us when she went to high school, was a joy and a blessing.

But events separated us. The charming hilltop house burned. What loving and generous hospitality we had shared there, often with Ripley friends! The family began visiting the doctor's sister, Virginia, who was living in Florida. On each trip the university town of Deland increased its appeal for both Eleanor and Mayo were nearing college age. The family found a house in Deland and moved there. Our paths continued to cross, but less often, as the years claimed our busy lives.

A few years later, family responsibilities ended, and alone, Bertha began doing mission work in Tampa. While there she met the John Turnbulls with their twenty one year old son Wallace. The Turnbulls were then on their way to Haiti to establish a mission. Bertha's old yen to answer, "Lord, here am I, send me" possessed her now with new urgency. In helping Mrs. Turnbull put together the things they would need in a primitive situation, Bertha pressed, "I wish you would pack me in your trunk."

A month later Bertha, now fifty nine, received a letter from the Turnbulls. They had acquired a small mountain site about fifteen miles up the mountain from Port-au-Prince for a mission and were planning to return to the States, leaving Wallace on the new field. They asked, could Bertha manage on forty dollars a month and come to help?

Relating all this to a friend on the street the next day, Bertha was visibly moved to see him count out sixty dollars and give them to her, saying it was the Lord's money. A little later a dentist promised to send her forty dollars a month. Convinced and joyful that this was the Lord's helping hand, Bertha counted her savings. There seemed to be enough. Reckoning that anything she might take with her would be useful, she filled a nail keg with cooking utensils, a hammer, some cord, soap, medicines, a mending kit, cloth remnants, and nails. She paid nine dollars for a two burner oil stove, bought a folding bed, added two quilts, a pillow, and her scant wardrobe. It cost her thirty dollars to ship her chattels to Haiti. When she got to Miami a friend gave her some money and the next day put her on the plane to Port-au-Prince. Less than a month after she reached Haiti, the man who had promised forty dollars a month, sent her his first and last check.

But Bertha was sure the Lord had brought her to Haiti and was as positive He would take care of her... she learned to be fed by the ravens.

Work Begins

With pick and shovel, Wallace had hewn out a footpath from the main mountain road to the three acre mission plot, and by the time the Turnbulls had departed and Bertha had arrived, he and a handful of the neighbors had begun work on a shelter.

And from the moment Granny had set foot in the small house across the road from the mission site, the curious and needy had begun coming. Rhoda Turnbull's ministry with swab and needle and physic had preceded her and gained fame, especially after Jean Baptiste hurt his leg digging out the road. Rhoda's use of an antiseptic and simple care prevented infection. It was common for a deep wound to rot away a hand or limb. Before Granny had removed the grime of her travel, she beheld her first loathsome case of yaws, followed by a child with its toes burned, another suffering with a sprouting bean in its ear, an old man in agony with an abscessed tooth—and on to the day's end. There seemed to be nothing but need!

Granny began holding dispensary three days a week under the avocado trees. Of the prattle of Creole she could understand not a word, though what she saw in their faces needed no translating. Half of them had worms. A fourth had yaws and ulcers. Yaws was a repulsive disfiguring disease. Another wasting disease, tuberculosis, often hidden by the family due to a prevailing stigma, claimed grievous numbers of emaciated bodies. Bellies of most of the children were distended by malnutrition and parasites. She seemed surrounded by dirt and sickness.

Granny worked there in the sun, sticky wisps of her auburn hair falling about her face, her clothing drenched with sweat. She had known disease and pain through the years in Missouri, Tennessee and Mississippi, but there was always a doctor, a hospital, drugs, and even surgery if the patient needed it.

Granny now saw a backward but simple hearted people living in mud huts with thatched roofs. She saw them cooking their mush and beans in round pots over evening fires. She heard them sing and dance as the beat of their drums punctured the lovely tropical nights. And as she moved among them, she knew they huddled for sleep on straw mats on the earth floor, with only their handwoven shoulder work baskets to cover threadbare bottoms against the cold. Nor doubt, did she, that each night stark fear also lay down beside them on those mats. She had cast her lot with a superstitious, witch doctor bound, evil spirit haunted people, who had a very real belief in magic and taboos, inherited from distant African forebears. And among them polygamy was the accepted way of life.

She struggled with the language. Indeed, she could see that the Haitian's afflictions of the flesh seemed less real than his torments of the mind. No amount of talk, with Madame Lacossade interpreting, could get through to them that there were parasites in the stream where the children romped and their mothers pounded the clothes and washed the vegetables, that this uncleanness could make the child sick. No, it was a curse. The spirits were

angry. The buried relative's spirit had followed the child home. He was being punished. If blood was showing, as from a cut, then that very real, invisible something was not pleased.

be persuaded to give up all this lore?

The mission's natal three acres was a haunted, abandoned site, the place of a witch doctor long since dead. No one doubted that his mysterious powers survived him. A donkey with a lighted candle on its head roamed the site at night. Children were warned not to graze their goats near the place or even pass by it. When Wallace and his helpers were excavating for the first rainwater reservoir, they unearthed goat skulls, earthen jars, colored beads, silver, dishes and other relics used by the Voodoo priests in their pacts with the spirits. Despite the unsavory legends surrounding this patch of ground, curiosity soon coaxed out the village men, clad in rags, their two foot sugarcane knives strapped to their sides. Ownership of a machete evinced far more self respect than raiment or being shod. Curiosity no less than the prospect of work for a few gourdes (a gourde was worth twenty cents) dispelled their fears. Their very willingness was the open sesame Wallace needed most. They not only helped him hew out the limestone; they taught him Creole.

Eleanor Comes to Visit

It was April when Granny arrived in Haiti. Her daughter Eleanor had taken a dim view of her mother undertaking a task so outlandish at fifty nine years of age. She herself was teaching, having applied to be sent to the mission field in Africa. With two degrees, she had prepared herself for rugged service, even to learning to pilot a small plane. Her mother's letters, few and irregular, left many unanswered questions. Came December and the Christmas vacation, Eleanor persuaded a friend to go with her to see how things were in Haiti.

Two rooms now graced the mission site, and Wallace was saving fifteen dollars a month out of his salary to buy cement. There was still no floor. The day the girls came, Granny had seen hordes of dispensary patients and Wallace had been out on the trails. In an old pickup truck, their only vehicle, they met the girls when their plane came in before dusk.

Wallace, tired and still surrounded by needy people at each day's end, had hardly given himself time to eat or sleep for weeks. "He rarely helped with household chores," Granny recalled, "especially with bringing in water. When the girls came, he couldn't do enough for me. He kept everything on the place filled with water. I began to wonder which one it was. Then it became clear that it was Eleanor."

For a Christmas gift to her mother, Eleanor had spent hours preparing nuts and fruits, then mixing and baking a fruitcake to bring with her to Haiti. To mellow the cake, she wrapped it in several layers of cider soaked cheesecloth. After giving it, Eleanor was to understand later why her mother made more of the cheesecloth than the cake. As soon as the diminishing fruitcake permitted, the fragrant lengths of cheesecloth were carefully washed and cut up into sorely needed bandages for the dispensary.

For this trip, Eleanor also paid forty dollars for a new suit After Wallace took her to a Voodoo dance close to the mission, she remarked on the way home, "Never again will I pay forty dollars for a suit."

Wallace and Eleanor Are Wed

T he following August, Wallace and Eleanor were married. Mrs. Rudolph Rosebrough of DeLand, Florida, gave Eleanor her trousseau. Friends gathered on the site of an unfinished chapel with a dirt floor and no windows. They came up from Port-au-Prince, from the embassy, the consulate, and other posts high and low. Pastor Marc stood as best man and the young couple pledged their vows with the western sky as a backdrop. And about fifteen hundred guests enjoyed Granny's wedding cookies and punch afterward.

The couple started housekeeping in those first unfinished rooms (now a part of the lower level of the house) which were shelter from the sun and the violent and sudden tropical storms. Already Granny's flowers and bushes half covered the sides, and hibiscus bloomed at the door.

Granny had visited the northwest peninsula and now decided to get a little church and dispensary started on that remote part of the island. She chose Anse Rouge, a village on the coast, seventy miles from Port-au-Prince as the crow flies. Her only choice of travel was by truck, either through deep mud or thick dust, depending on the season, loaded with people, animals and produce. After eight to ten hours of this, she had to sail from Gonaïves to St. Marc, a trip of eight to thirty hours. Granny resorted to these modes of travel during the eighteen months she spent with the people of Anse Rouge. Each time she went by boat she found a colorful character aboard whom she remembers as Madame Sidoine.

Granny chuckled as she usually does when she has a good story. "Madame Sidoine arrived at the dock well before the boat departure time. It had a schedule of two or three trips a week along the northern side of the bay, but, as they do in Haiti, they go by the sun. One goes aboard and waits. Greeting the skipper jovially, soon Madame Sidoine came leisurely aboard. An angular, good natured woman laden with two baskets, one filled with peanuts, the other with gay colored scarves which she would sell to the passengers, she squeezed down between a dock worker and an old man. Bag and baggage of the passengers consisted of everything they carry on camions—turkeys, chickens, fruits and vegetables, charcoal, baked goods, fish, anything they had bought or had for sale. Not an inch of space was unclaimed. The Haitian has precious little of the world's goods, but if he goes anywhere, he takes most of what he has with him. Madame Sidoine was different in that she was a vendor who made the boat her home. She hawked her wares from time to time, and when the boat docked at St. Marc, she got off to add to her stock, this time palm leaf mats and sandals.

"We didn't reach Anse Rouge until about noon the next day. The moon was bright as day. That night we learned that Madame Sidoine was a good story teller. At that time my Creole served only in small group exchanges and most of her raciness was lost on me. She never lacked a responsive audience. Once, while telling a story, she got herself untied, potty in hand, lifted one knee, went on with her story, then emptied the potty in the sea as casually as if she had adjusted an earring.

"A voyage by boat is always relieved by stops, and there is a great amount of laughter and singing and chattering. No one can forget the brilliance of the stars and their reflection in the rippling water, or the splendor of the moon."

Atrèl

"Getting the work started at Atrèl, the little farm community inland from Anse Rouge, was a joyless excursion into purgatory. Purgatory would have no new cunning to vex the spirit, flay the soul, or scorch the flesh for any who dwelt there. A two year drought deadened every living thing. Coconut palms gasped for rain, the ground around baked and cruelly fissured.

"Little port sailing vessels would bring outsiders, mostly tobacco speculators, and drums of drinking water from Gonaïves. The only well for nine hundred villagers had been drilled years before by American Seabees. Now village police had to stand by until the children could fill their gourds. Every hut and yard was fenced around to keep out the pigs and goats, or they would destroy the mud masonry walls and harass the occupants. The dogs, village scavengers, suffered tortuous thirst and searched incessantly for any morsel of refuse. Out of pity I often set my pan of grimy bath water out for these animals, and let the squash vine die instead.

"This was before I had acquired a fair speaking facility with Creole. Madame Lacossade had accompanied me as interpreter. She tried to get across the story of the man who dreamed he saw heaven and hell. How well she did, I couldn't be sure then, but some seed fell on good ground.

" 'The people in both places had long forks fastened to their arms and sat at tables laden with food. In heaven the people were all happy and well fed, for they fed each other across the table. In hell they fought and starved rather than cooperate.' "

The seed that were planted did come up and bear fruit for there is now a church, enlarged the third time, a large school, ten teachers (six of whom Granny continues to support) and several outstations. Many of the teenage boys walk four hours each day just to get an education.

Sunstroke

The last time Granny made the trip by boat to St. Marc, she intended to get the truck from there to Port-au-Prince. She had exhausted herself rounding out the work at Anse Rouge and training a native leader and helpers. Her thoughts had turned anxiously to Fermathe for it was time for the arrival of her first grandchild. Accustomed as she was to the heat, she nonetheless felt strangely unable to feel comfortable the entire trip. She did not know it then, but she had suffered a sunstroke.

"My clothes were wet, my face was burning, and everything seemed unbearably hot. Vaguely aware that we had reached St. Marc, it wasn't until the boat bumped the wharf and all on board, people and animals swaying their hot sticky bodies helplessly en masse, like a tray of baby chicks too long under the heat lamp, did I realize I was more limp than the rest. The ends of ropes flew over our heads, the boat heaved and the water churned below. I was carried along with the crowd ashore. The dusty sloping road uptown seemed unending. There were smells and I thought I had not the strength to take another step. Women were hawking their coconuts and fish and wares. They banged on their pots with the usual, 'Three gourdes, Madame!' I knew I must get out of the sun... I must have fainted, for when I awoke some kind people had taken me in. The room was clean and so was the bed on which I lay. The windows were open, the strong sunlight excluded by partly closed blinds. From time to time a hot breeze brought in the smells from the hot dusty road. When I raised my head the swimming pulled me back. How long I lay lifeless and listless I did not know, but within a day or so I began to think that Eleanor would be frantic but there was no way to let her know where I was.

"There was a little narrow gauge train that had one passenger car which would offer easier travel than the open truck to Port-au-Prince, although the little train went only to the outskirts of the city. A small steam engine with a wood-fed boiler pulled three or four warped sided cars and a little open passenger car along forty miles of track. The train was somewhat of a hazard to the countryside, for sometimes sparks from the burning wood would fall on the thatched roofs of huts along the way and destroy them. Hardly able to hold up my head, my good Samaritan friends at my insistence put me on the little train. It was a onetime experience for me, for the next year the wooden cars could no longer be repaired, wood was too scarce to fire the boiler, and the little engine was retired. The tracks have since been taken up and sold for scrap iron, and maybe, wobbly as I was, that trip gave me the distinction of being the last American who traveled on Haiti's passenger train.

"Eleanor had checked with the police and was soon at the station to take me up the mountain where it was cooler and I could rest. It was such a rare occurrence for me to be interned by illness, Eleanor tells it: 'She hovered between this world and the next for awhile and at length recovered, and her pace hasn't slackened since.'"

Healing and Teaching at Fermathe

Granny's first grandson was six weeks old and the work at Fermathe was growing. All agreed that there she was needed most. She paid forty dollars for a little piece of mountain slope adjoining the Turnbulls, house. Wallace had the site leveled, a retaining wall

built and then Granny's house. She could now carry on her clinic in a room, a stone enclosure that made her feel that she had come into her own with a touch of rank, had there been any other than the witch doctor to challenge.

The sick there were always. And much of the sickness that came was beyond her ability to alleviate. Stitching up a wound, she did often. Repairing torn ear lobes and other rents and tears, even reducing simple fractures and getting good results never fazed Granny. But there were strangulating hernias and abdominal emergencies that she knew she was powerless to help until there was a doctor and a hospital operating room. She also knew that she was getting many of the hopeless cases that the witch doctor declined to "cure". One little boy, a witch doctor's son, came hobbling up with toenails and fingernails so badly infected by chique fleas that some of his toes had sloughed off. This flea burrows under the skin around the toenails and develops its young in a sac which grows to about the size of a green pea. If not removed, the young will hatch and continue the infestation to the other toes. They itch outrageously and increase until they form ulcerated sores. The sensible thing to do is to dig out the first flea. Granny spent hours digging them all out. It took some heroics to rid this little boy, but it paved the way that years later brought his mother and two sisters to know the Lord and permit a public burning of their Voodoo charms.

In those early days, yaws was the disease most dreadful and there was not yet penicillin. Caused by an infectious organism that forms yellow crusty sores, if untreated it sometimes progressed to loss of fingers and toes resembling leprosy. The Negro slave is said to have brought it from Africa. The government program in 1950-52 eradicated this disease, as well as helped reduce malaria.

And there were worms, big and little, ulcers and itch and lice. There were boils to lance and teeth to pull. TB she could do little about. They were ashamed of the disease because it was regarded as a curse, and few admitted having it. Lusterless hair and eyes, dull expression, coughing and general weakness were evidence enough for diagnosis.

There were no facilities for laboratory examination, until that glad day in 1967 a rainbow arched over the mission: There was a doctor and rooms for a hospital. Add to the rejoicing the hopeful effort that now could be diverted to prevention. Who can calculate how much a parasite, poor nutrition, and an infection like TB or syphilis can sap a person's energy? To many, sickness is the norm, a lifelong thralldom. Lucky the Haitian who has only one disease. Then, who can blame him for being lackadaisical?

The great debilitator, before a law forbade bare feet on the streets and in the market places of Port-au-Prince, was hookworm.

The larvae of this little parasite enter through the skin of the feet, migrate through the bloodstream and lodge in the lungs, to be coughed up and swallowed. The adult parasites then feed on blood through the walls of the intestine. Wearing sandals has helped. But the problem will continue to be around until sanitary disposal of human excreta is a way of life on the island. As in most diseases of the tropics, prevention is better than cure. Since Haiti had a limited public health program, the best next step was to train native nurses and midwives, who could do the groundwork for rural health education.

Without education it would be like attempting to pull a load uphill with only one ox hitched in a yoke designed for a team. No amount of talk could persuade an illiterate person to adopt ways that his social situation did not make clear. Only as his standard rose would there be better sanitation. How right were the Pan Am health engineers who stopped at the mission: "We can build latrines all over the world but they are useless until people are educated to use them." Does Stalien, who keeps clean the one across from the hospital where the patients wait, not have to show them every day?

Granny's techniques, she admitted, during those early years would not have won the plaudits of her nursing supervisor, but even creosote performed not a few miracles. Sometimes a diagnosis was elusive. Some questions needed answers if the right thing were to be given to swallow. But getting a history from one of them was like bowing away from an encore. To every question the response would be yes, no matter what it was. They were merely polite and courteous. In the same way, they would come asking to be converted. They were trying to please. The missionary wanted them to accept the New Way. It was hard for her to be sure who was sincere. Usually she could tell after the amen was said, if their first question was, "Will you give me a job? My cow got in my neighbor's garden and I must pay twelve gourdes. Will you lend it to me?"; or, if the worship service had preceded the public clinic, scores of upraised hands would avow they were ready to be converted for a dose of castor oil. They had learned more than anything else that the foreign missionary who had come to them wanted them to be converted. To refuse was to be rude to a guest.

Who could blame them if the torments of body outweighed the gentil homme? So they came—halt, lame, blind, bent with rheumatism, covered with yellow pustules—oh, so long before they got the hospital. When the doctor came, scores increased to hundreds!

Granny continued to help, keeping water hot for sterilization, swabbing arms for injections, never able to supply enough sponges and dressings. Dr. Thebaud did the treating, lancing, removing foreign bodies, repairing hernias, and the pulling of teeth until another glad day brought a dentist, Dr. Nazon, a volunteer who helped out over twenty years.

"The routine of seeing an unending stream of bodies undernourished, ailing with half a dozen diseases, would be too much for most American doctors. Day after day after day. And the smells! Always the smells, theirs and ours to counteract. Theirs were for the most part those they could not help, for bad smells are to them taboo, dangerous and unhealthy. So it is to their credit that they do a commendable job of keeping themselves clean, walking miles as they do for a gourdful of water," Granny contended for them.

It was one of those times with Dr. Pressoir, when his usual aplomb had deserted him and Granny could tell that his sufferance had reached the danger point. The lab technician did not come that day, and the doctor had to do her work. He and Granny had stoically made it through the usual excising, stitching, swabbing, dressing, lancing, anointing, and pulling, before he went to the lab. He tackled sputum, blood, urine, feces. Before he did the last, there were ten new cases of TB, one tetanus, one meningitis, four hepatitis. Then began the hunt for parasites. The Creole word for stool is selle. For salt it is sel. For saddle it is selle. All pronounced the same. "Let's see, who's first?" and an anemic woman laid her offering before the doctor—a handful of sea salt which she used in cooking. It was tied in an old rag. Next, an emaciated youth shifted an old wooden saddle from the floor to the table. The two women next were arguing and expostulating. If the doctor had asked her for this to make a fetish against her sickness, then why not include some from every member of the family and keep the whole family healthy? Her bowl contained samples from them all! Too tired to see any humor in this situation, the doctor turned to Granny and said "See if you can make them understand to bring a specimen tomorrow', and he left. But tomorrow brought confusion too. Mrs. P. had told a patient to bring a little poupou in a matchbox; she brought the box with each match carefully swabbed in *selle*.

Since many of the patients live a day's journey away, perhaps two or three days, the family usually comes along. The TB ward and the convalescent shelter was the next great blessing. Keeping sixty six patients at a time for several weeks, hundreds are treated during a year. Very little of the cost is paid by the patients. But each is required to pay something, no matter how little. This was the principle that proved sound in those early years, later helped the hospital, and always preserved the patient's self respect. And, although it remained more principle than practice—a sufferer too poor to pay is not refused—a certain amount of labor generally came with cure and keep. If he was a bed patient, his relatives took the bedclothes and the piece of soap Granny gave them, went down to the spring and washed. They would bring scrawny chickens, eggs that were fresh only a week ago, now and then bananas or roasting ears. All chickens were scrawny and an egg was an egg, and it was their way of expressing thanks.

Yet, as Granny and Wallace and Eleanor and the others labored to bring healing, they were daily overwhelmed by that which neither antiseptic nor analgesic could allay, those fears that imprisoned the minds of most on the mountain. Who had not seen them seized with trembling, a clammy sweat popping out on face and hands? This symptom bared an unmistakable sense of impending doom. Awful fears cramped their very souls. They had violated a taboo. Inexorable, absolute, inescapable destruction awaited. There were times when no other explanation than fear could be made for a person's death. When Bertha Halstenberg was turned back from an appointment to serve in Africa, and felt that she had been denied her dedication to help people who lived in darkness and fear, little did she dream then in what an incredible counterpart of Africa would she find fulfillment and redeem her pledge, Lord, send me!

To the fears of real life there was added that dread shadow of fear, the taboo, which had held primitive minds in bondage from man's emergence from the jungle. It was taboo to touch the dead, or to walk near a grave at night. It was taboo to let a child go to the cemetery to bury a brother, lest the sibling's spirit follow the child home and take him to the cemetery to live also. A young mother who loses her babe must tie a string about her toe to prevent her milk from going to her head to cause fever and delirium. If one mixes hot and cold, sickness will result. A girl does not take a drink of cold water while ironing, nor does she get wet or cold when having her hair straightened with a charcoal heated comb. Such imprudence may cause illness years later. Never tell how many pigs or chickens or even children one has, lest the spirits hear and take one. Say, "I have five children and one piece," and the spirits will be fooled.

More devastating than taboo was the curse.

Haiti is the only place in the world where a wife can fool a husband who has been away from home over a year. Pregnancy may last for years. An enemy prevails on the houngan to "tie" the child inside the mother. Maricia had helped at the mission and had parted from the man who fathered her two children. He had another family and her Christian relatives prevailed on her to leave. After about a year she became pregnant. Meanwhile, the man had been converted and wanted to marry Maricia. Both insisted the child had been "planted" more than a year before and he had made fetishes to "tie" it. Only recently did he return to the witch doctor to "untie" the child so it could grow.

How dark and complex the web of Voodoo that controlled their lives!

Too weary to take off her clothes, often Granny would lie across her bed at night and hear only the distant beat of the Voodoo drums. Health, she was convinced, is more than the absence of disease... oh, much more. He had said, *I came that ye might have life, abundant life...*

To relieve their pain, to restore them to their gardens and patches, to teach them to read and write...."Oh, Lord what I do for their tortured bodies is just for now. If I teach them to know the Lord and in Him to have courage to fear no evil, it will go on into their children's lives."

They were gaining ground against Voodooism, despite all the superstition. There were Catule and Meristaine and Toulon and Antoine... who could doubt God's miracle of grace in them?

Granny never forgot one of the Turnbulls, back country treks. While "manning" the mission alone and caring for her two little grandsons, she faced crisis with six month old Sandy.

Sandy

Eleanor was preparing to go with Wallace on one of those back country treks. TiWally, fair and red haired three year old, and Sandy, not six months old, would stay with Granny. Sandy, by mild pediatric collation, was a frail baby. Because he was sickly, Granny felt that Eleanor should not go. But she knew she was going anyway. The morning came. As Eleanor climbed up beside Wallace, she reminded Granny that the doctor said to boil carrots and give the baby the carrot water in his bottle, and Madame Saut Lous', daughter would be over to help.

Not that caring for the two babies while manning the mission alone would be tribulation more extreme than bumping and retching over the hot, dry northwest, carrying a bedroll and camp kit through thick brush and thorny vines and swarms of insects, eating rice and beans with the flies and natives. It would be two weeks, maybe longer, before she would see Eleanor and Wallace again. And no way of communicating. What if the baby became gravely ill? Her thoughts plummeted. She was twenty miles from Port-au-Prince and the doctor. What if the baby should die? Dear Lord, she would have to bury him! Gathering up both children, she crowded into the next camion to Petionville and there bought some Similac. When they got back to the mission, she boiled rice and fixed a feeding of Similac and the warm rice water. She kept the baby with her, and tended him, day and night. After two days, the doctor, uneasy that she had not come, came up to see about Sandy. He was better.

Years later, when Sandy had grown up to be healthy and strong and was in college, he wrote about the childhood he enjoyed living in two cultures:

> Inside our home we are American—speaking English and surrounded by good English books and periodicals, with American and European friends frequenting our home for short and extended visits. Outside the home is the world I've known and loved as my world from childhood. A Haitian bonne (child nurse) and mountain playmates taught me the native Creole before my parents of the other world could teach me English. It was the familiar and smiling world of the people of Haiti that I knew and loved. The dried herring and cornmeal eaten with fingers among friendly neighbor children was more of a special treat than the ice cream my mom made so much fuss about. The children with grubby dirty hands would break a piece of their half baked sweet potato and give it to me. A penny pancake of grated manioc root was always shared. I knew their love and unselfishness. Only when there was talk about it being time for worm medicine (because of supposed tropical parasites taking my appetite) would I stay away from the big pots of native food cooking over wood fires for the children's canteen. I knew I should not be overstuffed at dinner time or they would blame the intestinal parasites and bring out the bitter stinking vermifuge dropped

in castor oil. There was never a shortage of playmates. Christophe was one of my favorites. He was two years older than I and as much a hero to me as his namesake Henri Christophe was to the slaves he helped to free from French domination. I thought he was fortunate because he didn't have to be yakked at about proper use of silverware or table manners (he used no table). His mother never told him to take his feet off the furniture for there was nothing but a rolled up straw mat and a hollowed out tree trunk for furniture in his house. At his house we were never punished because we tracked in mud—his house had a dirt floor. His dad wasn't always barking at him to hold his shoulders straight. Christophe had beautiful posture because since he was little he had been carrying tall cans of water balanced on his head. Another reason I envied him was that he didn't have to stand on his head to scrub the ring from the bathtub. His routine bathing was what our household considered a holiday outing. He hiked down to the mountain stream and there splashed and frolicked with other children for his bath.

At the age of four and one half I met a halfway world... the children I came to know at Madame Scott's kindergarten. This was nine miles down the mountain from the mission in the residential suburb of Petionville. To this kindergarten went the children of doctors, lawyers, merchants, the educated well-to-do. Most of these children were light mulattos—so far removed from the world I'd known that the entire school year passed before I could believe they were Haitians. They were beautiful, soft faced children with individually tailored clothes and hair styles, impeccable French and polished manners. I knew from the beginning that I was a 'foreigner' among them. Here I learned French, showed interest in drawing, and delighted to be a comedian. I loved Mrs. Scott though I never learned the tunes to her many French songs. I found her husband, Captain Scott, much more interesting. He kept fighting cocks for a hobby and rather than polishing a little boy with stilted French manners, he'd explain the merits of his prize cocks. At four p.m. I'd hitchhike home on crowded public trucks, back to my two worlds.

Christophe usually had the earthworms dug when I got home. This was the condition under which he could use one of the fishhooks. Inspired by a United Nations project, my dad had made a fine fish pool, a demonstration to the mountain people for raising fish as a source of protein for their children. Among the happiest of my childhood memories are these late afternoons or early Saturday mornings spent fishing with Christophe or my grandmother.

...The halfway world continued as I entered regular school at College Tête de l'Eau. This was a private school operated by the French wife of the Minister of Finance. Here I continued my education from eight a.m. until four p.m. each day, October through July.

When I was nine years old my parents took our family to the United States... It all seemed like a dream... Elevators and escalators—telephones that worked—organized traffic—smooth, multilaned highways! The people spoke of hospitals and doctors as faraway, mysterious untouchable things. In Haiti I had watched operations, seen doctors struggle to make a newborn breathe, seen teeth pulled by the dozen. I'd held flashlights and lanterns during blackouts so doctors could sew deep wounds. In the United States I was impressed how the people tiptoed around funeral homes and whispered about death. I thought them strange to consider death fearful and unreal—almost as though they tried to deny it. In Haiti, I'd dug from the missionary barrels the threadbare garments for burying the poor. I'd learned that the stronger clothes must be kept for the living.

Driving through the countryside I saw Dog and Cat Hospital signs. I couldn't reconcile this with the worry I'd seen on my parents faces in Haiti as they'd discuss children with tuberculosis or other illnesses and no funds to buy the needed drugs... True, I saw starving people, blind and crippled beggars surrounding our car whenever we stopped at Port-au-Prince, swollen children dying from protein deficiency, little ones abandoned at our door. Three hurricanes in ten years devastated the mountain area. Instead of regarding it as too ugly to see, I was put to work in relief efforts.

Granny's Other World

Not a day since Granny arrived in Haiti had hunger and need failed to stir her compassion. The hurt was more exquisite because her own life up until that time had been blessed with plenty. In her Midwest German home bounty came to the table five times a day; she married a widower whose acres and manner of life in north Mississippi spelled plenitude from any side of the rambling hilltop home whence Holdeman hospitality was extended. Storerooms beyond the house contained hundreds of cans and jars filled with soup mixture, fruits and vegetables, preserves and jellies; bushels of sweet potatoes, bins of Irish potatoes, peanuts, popcorn. In the cellar, ahead of the first frost, pumpkins, apples and turnips shared space with green tomatoes to ripen on their vines overhead. Hardy enough to withstand the cold of Southern winters, shallots, turnip greens and collards were left to be gathered as needed. No neighbor's excelled the hams, shoulders and middlings, the souse and sausage cured in the Holdeman smokehouse. And in some north Mississippi homes, fleecy blankets still come out of moth balls on chill wintry nights—wool shorn from the Holdeman flock, shipped uncarded to a Chatham, North Carolina mill to be woven into luxuriously soft plaids, pastels and solids. Not a few brides from families close to this family had one of these blankets among their wedding gifts. Some old-time residents of the hill section recall a fine race horse or two and even peacocks that graced the Holdeman hacienda.

Not that Bertha basked in the lap of all this plenty; forsooth, no farm woman outdid her in turning off work. No neighbor for miles around failed to learn from her, how to can and cook and sew and serve better meals in simple farm homes. Nor could the banker's and merchant's wife in Ripley, the county seat, or the teacher's and doctor's wife in Booneville, the adjoining county seat, forget those times when Bertha entertained. Near catastrophe overtook one midsummer luncheon under the oaks. Twenty odd ladies in cool voiles and crisp muslins were being served outdoor party fare of stuffed tomatoes, spiced pears, condiments, hot rolls, and potato salad. Heartiest part of the menu, the salad contained among other delicacies, three dozen hardboiled eggs, and was mixed with the hostess, best homemade dressing. It required such a large salver, she commissioned her young son to take it up to the grove on his farm wagonette, or small dray. A moment before the salad reached its destination, perverseness took over, the salver began sliding, and before anyone could rescue it, completely upturned and emptied its contents on the ground. For years afterward the hostess and her friends enjoyed quipping about the salad that was!

Converts

Granny reached back. "In my first year while I had my Jamaican interpreter, Dorcilia came from Bongar to the mission to beg. A basket on her head, one child tied to her back and another in her arms, she responded to our explanation of the gospel and convinced us that her understanding and faith were real. When she returned to her home accompanied by some Christians we sent, she asked the men to chop down her Voodoo banana grove. And despite threatening messages, which she left with the Lord, she brought others and used her little home for meetings. Her testimony was so genuine that she became a growing Christian witness, and later was one of our first demi-missionaries.

"New converts need to prove that they have a new life in Christ," she continued. "It's not uncommon for a penitent to be looking for more powerful charms. So the deacons question him to determine if his change is genuine. First he must spend a long time in the believers' class. He must also answer rightly a simple catechism before he may go into the baptismal waters. Less often now do we have to contend with shilly-shallying. The local leaders have taken over the candidates, class, and when a would be member like scatterbrained Crevelia comes before these lay leaders, she and the church are spared. Twice Crevelia, came before Wallace, but was not accepted. Finally, the native workers passed her. But, obviously pregnant as she came out of the baptismal waters, her lover an unbeliever, rejoicing straightway gave way to prayer and supplication."

Humility

Now that the mission had grown, and others had taken over most of the work, how did Granny feel?

When a work is once begun
Never leave it till it's done
Be the labor great or small
Do it well or not at all

This was the way she had been brought up. But she was not reflecting with pride on the accomplishments of her work. Instead, she measured her inadequacy in the face of the limitless undone tasks that confronted the mission. She had prayed all her life to be exempt from pride. Blessed are the meek to her meant those who have such reverent lowliness of spirit, their legacy is God's earth and its needs. How well she knew that the heart's gates will never open to let compassion flow through if pride is the gatekeeper.

"In Haiti it is as real a problem as anywhere else. In our early days here a Haitian male wearing shoes looked down on his barefoot neighbor. The girls want a wig and purse and clothes. They will do without food to have these things.

"Tradition forbids the male to do work that has always been done by woman. When Simon's wife left him with four little children, his mother came to help out. Seeing her walk to market with forty or fifty pounds of vegetables on her head, we would urge Simon to carry the water to ease her lot. No! Like any other Haitian male, he would ride his horse, shoes on his feet, while the mother walked barefooted with a load on her head that even he could hardly lift.

"Once a child has learned to read, he refuses to do menial jobs. I use the new converts' class to teach them, and I never spare them in teaching lessons against the sin of pride. Also, I turn down those who come to learn English so they can go to the States to make some money. Pierre I did teach. A leaf doctor and recognized leader, he came with the fixed notion of making a teacher of himself. No pretender, he tucked his pride in his pocket and gamely started in the learners' class and plugged along until he could read. Some are so good at memorizing, they can repeat long passages without actually having learned to read, but hold the book to appear that they are reading. Again, some who have never seen anything on paper, see nothing at all. In those early days we tried to use some of our pictures for teaching the adults Bible stories, but because they were as strange objects from outer space, we had to put them away."

Faithfulness

Granny now began dark-fielding a virtue no less estimable than humility—faithfulness. The Haitian Independence Day is the first of January. "Their celebration of this national holiday is next to Mardi Gras in determined festive-making. The hospital aides have been coming all morning for advance pay. Even Madame Lamothe, the laboratory technician, has twice gone down to Wallace's office for her pay, although tomorrow is dispensary day. All will be away from their posts. Even the doctors are late. And patients will have walked perhaps two days to get here. How can we tell a man to take his sick wife back home and return with her after the holiday? How can the doctors do their work without tests? Ingrained with tradition, superstition, and resistance to change, they are harder to train in the Christian ethic than teaching an old dog to leave his bone at the door rather than bury it. And we've now had them a full generation. I start with the children. Eleanor works with the youth. Finally, Wallace gets them as adults, when we look forward to a crop of acutely needed leaders and pastors for the churches... but their number is multiplying," she admitted.

Josèf had returned and was waiting patiently to get Granny's attention. Could she send some more things up to the tearoom?

"Pickles, jams, candies, and apple sauce go faster than I can find jars for them. Last month, friends on the Gitmo base sent over two big boxes of empty jars wrapped in old newspapers which were almost as rich a boon as the jars."

Because Granny could sell Christmas candles made from recycled wax aprons, fashioned from remnants, pickles and preserves and chocolates and peanut brittle which seldom lasted the day in the tearoom, so could the rural women. Eager to earn enough now to keep their children in school, the women came to learn how to hem and embroider tea napkins, aprons, smocks, ponchos and the like for the outlet shop. One young girl walked nine miles each day up from Petionville to learn embroidery and sewing, so priceless was the chance to learn through the mission outlet. They learned to dip and fashion candles. The candles then needed holders for the tourist trade so the choir director and a Sunday school teacher of the Fermathe church became adept in metal craft. This requires some resourcefulness in replenishing raw material. When they salvaged a wrecked publique from the ravine below the mission it was a bonanza. (The publique was coming down the mountain in heavy fog and rain one night sans windshield wipers with thirteen people aboard. It plunged all the way down the mountainside all surviving save two.) What a treasure trove one old car junk yard in the States would be for Fermathe metalworkers!

Josèf had returned again, this time with a batch of mail. She began sorting the letters and Christmas cards, each sender's name evoking a new chuckle and something dear she wanted to share. "We get them on into March, depending on the vagaries of post office clerks from there to here."

While others double-check addresses and zip codes, Granny miles above Port-au-Prince receives her mail addressed GRANNY HOLDEMAN, Port-au-Prince or simply, GRANNY, HAITI. She answers every card and letter. More likely on the back side or inside turned out, and if nothing better, a scrap of envelope on which she relates something warm and personal.

There were checks in many of them. Fifteen dollars from Roanoke, Indiana, $50.00 Akron, Ohio, $25.00 Greensburg, North Carolina, $20.00 Rockford, Illinois, $100.00 Fort Lupton, Colorado, $25.00 Augusta, Michigan, $275.00 for which an Auburn, Indiana, church sold a motorcycle to help Granny, $10.00 from a newspaper reporter who talked with her once, $73.00 Coon Rapids, Minnesota, $25.00 Detroit, Michigan $400.00 Arvada, Colorado, $125.00 Suffolk, Virginia, $25.00 Wilcox, Arizona, $500.00 memorial, Excelsior Minnesota $15.00 Wichita, Kansas, $50.00 Fort Wayne, Indiana, $20.00 Walnut, Mississippi. Most remembered a time when she had visited in their church, had heard her talk of TiFam or André, and display Voodoo charms. All had been unforgettably touched or fascinated by this intrepid Granny, Saint of Haiti!

Dieula had now come, and was waiting for a break in Granny's story. The sausage was ready... With a little cooing sound as if in reverie still, Granny got up and went to show the girls in the kitchen how to bag and store fresh meat.

On Deputation

Weaks Martin drove 1000 miles again to see Granny when she was on her last trip to Tulsa and Ft. Worth—her last mission conference in 1979.

D uring her first ten years on the mission field, not once did Granny make a visit back to the States. The work had grown. Several churches in the States were including Haiti in their mission support, and the mission board felt that Granny should visit some of the churches. If it would be good for the mission, yes, Granny would go.

In the airport at Miami she sat waiting for her flight to Michigan to be called. Suddenly, homesickness for Haiti engulfed her. She sat shaking her head so sorrowfully that another traveler came over and touched her. "Are you all right?" she asked anxiously. Granny regained her poise and smiled. Soon the other woman found herself a willing captive of this hitherto forlorn but now animated aging woman until her own flight was called. When she left, Granny's spirit was recharged and ready for her first ambassadorial assignment for Haiti.

Granny's first talk was before a midweek prayer meeting group. She poured her heart out about the Haitians, their illiteracy and illegitimacy, their demons and darkness, their charms and curses. Surely she had prevailed on some to purvey and pray. She sat down and the service was ended. Everybody was leaving, so she started out too, her heart heavy that no one seemed in the mood to hear or heed. Then, hopeful that the four tarrying in the vestibule were sensitive sympathizers ready to pray for and support the work, she moved expectantly in their direction.

One ventured toward her. "Tell us, Mrs. Holdeman, if you don't mind, how old you are. And what do you do to keep your hair its natural color?"

This happened not only once, but following her next engagement, and then a third time. Distressed that nothing she was saying seemed to matter, she concluded that she might as well go back to Haiti, her efforts wasted. Several more places were on her schedule, so she decided to try once more. This time she spared herself by prefacing her talk with, "I'm sixty nine years old. The Lord has not seen fit to adorn my years with white or silvery glory, and if you will forgive His impertinence, it could be that my reddish braids fare better in a land where a woman wears either a multicolored kerchief or a French hairdo, depending on her social status." Granny continued, with color. "If she's a city lady, her clothes might come from Paris or London or New York, and she might live in a cantilevered house of contemporary architecture, speak French and dine and dance with other city friends. If she's peasant, as ninety five percent are, she will wear a carefully coiled cloth atop her head to balance her basket of vegetables or her gourd of water from the spring. She will climb the steep mountainside to her one-room hut roofed with banana leaves and palm fronds and grass, and walled with mud over a framework of flimsy poles."

Granny thereafter captivated her hearers. They listened intently as she regaled them with stories about Haiti. Most were moved and afterward gathered around her with questions. Often apologetic for shallowness in their own Christian life, they would ask to become a part of the mission outreach. Thus they became Granny's friends, were put on her prayer list and on her mailing list.

It was another ten years before Granny went to the States again. Her deputation stops took nine months. When she celebrated her eightieth birthday, American friends made much of the milestone.

Still no silver-tongued orator, this slight, plain, matter-of-fact woman in clothes that had forgotten their era of chic, nonetheless was something of a spellbinder. Her voice rode with such fervor and empathy that one forgot the characteristic twang and was caught up by the imperviousness of her message. At a Michigan church, the midweek offering had been designated for the radio program. After Granny spoke, someone rose and opined that Haiti needed it more than the radio program and it was voted changed to Haiti. Whereupon another rose and moved that now a special offering be taken for Haiti; the motion was passed and promptly acted upon.

Again and again Granny was given a check with, "Get something for yourself, Granny." "Oh, this will feed ten children a month," she would reply... or "This will pay tuition for twenty children for half a year." It was impossible to give this dear selfless mortal anything. Yet wherever she went, someone could mark the beginning of a new spiritual life from her visit. "Nearest thing to an angel we ever had in our home," wrote one.

Carrying her own suitcase, Granny traveled by bus. An Arizona hostess met her bus one afternoon, surprised that an eighty-year-old woman would be traveling across country alone. Sure that she was tired, Mrs. Ham asked if she would like to take a nap before dinner. She said, "Oh, no, I never lie down in the daytime." She wanted to talk about Haiti.

Another friend (Sally Fitzsimmons) marveled at her stamina. "She had spoken in Decatur, Illinois, that morning, Danville that night, taken a bus at midnight and arrived in Detroit at four in the morning... with no fear whatsoever for her safety."

Not every schedule turned out as planned. She had only one more engagement with a church in Flint, Michigan, then she would start homeward to Haiti. With a certain elation she boarded her bus, and had traveled through several towns before things seemed a little strange. She discovered that she was heading southeast to Detroit, not east to Flint. Unable to conceal her frustration, she left her seat and imparted her predicament to the driver. He looked at her, then at her Haitian-made suitcase of salvaged flattened oil cans (common in Haiti). He asked her where she was from, as if trying to decide that she might be slightly touched. When she told him Haiti, his silence then disturbed her. Although she continued to insist that she must go to Flint, he soothingly advised her to stay on the bus. Even after she reached Detroit and started for the phone booth in the bus depot, the driver seemed worried about her. To reach Flint for her speaking engagement seventy five miles back north was now impossible. After her call to cancel her talk, she thought, oh well, she was heading south and she really didn't need all those old bones and fetishes and relics in her bag any longer. But she dared not open that bag to dispose of them. That driver might not be the only one chary about her.

Most friends remember Granny's zest and youthfulness. For several years a Sunday school class in Huntington, Indiana, had written her letters, signing them, the True Blue Sunday School Class. The time came when Granny could visit the group. When she arrived at the home of Mrs. Paul and was greeted by several senior citizens, she stood speechless for a moment. Then someone said, "You must have thought we were teenagers!" Granny cried, "I did!" Everybody laughed and thereafter their letters were signed, Your Teenagers.

Young people enjoyed her. She would be on the floor working puzzles, around the fire popping corn and telling stories about Lizard and TiFam to the Sherwood children, or having as much fun at the zoo with the lions and chimpanzees as the youngest of the Hendrickson children, whom she then took for a ride on the little train. The Stafford youngsters, Syndy and Casey, had no less fun than Granny cruising about town in their sportive red convertible. And no one sat more breathlessly enthralled with Cinarama's Seven Wonders of the World than she. She came out remembering to write missionary friends in India and Japan and Egypt that she had seen the marvels of their part of the world, although she knew she would never go there.

Such times as these she seemed to forget Haiti, its hunger and its need, then someone might hear her murmur at the dinner table with a little forgivable sigh of relief that she could enjoy eating "since no one was watching through the window." She found meat with fat on it especially appetizing. If the beef animals in Haiti are fat when they start to market, they will have walked it off by the time they reach the slaughter. Beef cattle, raised mostly on the southern peninsula, are driven on foot a hundred miles to the Port-au-Prince market.

No one failed to notice Granny's uncheerfulness about waste. She picked up slightly bent nails from a construction site, saved yards of wrapping twine, turned off lights, and bathed in a halffilled tub. While a guest in a home, she might teach her hostess how to convert surplus bacon fat into soap. "I've never seen so much bacon fat going to waste in America! How I wish I could take it all back to Haiti!"

While in the Front Lake, Washington, home of the Underwoods, a small sewing bee developed around some discarded Army tarpaulins which were ripped up and re-sewed into a hundred sturdy school bags to go with Granny back to Haiti.

One day she picked up a couple of old horseshoes which she asked to take to her grandsons, and her host obligingly collected several more for that nothing like it freight pool, bound for Haiti from Miami.

Seeing the kudzu vine (originally planted along highways for erosion control) spanning gullies, overspreading undergrowth, and festooning trees in a greedy canopy of green, Granny was sure that here was both erosion control and nutrient rich grazing for Haiti's goats. Five pounds of seed and considerably more kudzu roots were trussed and added to Granny's burgeoning luggage. Her green thumb also had her digging iris rhizomes from the George Peeks, iris beds, lily bulbs and raspberry plants from the neighbors, gardens.

What could she do when she passed curb markets flaunting the season's new apple crop? How poignant the memory of making applesauce and apple butter in that big farmhouse kitchen of her childhood! Not surprised to hear her betray this transient longing, in a small voice as if soothing herself, "Apples don't grow in Haiti, you know," the Johnsons solved everything one bright autumn day by stopping at the last roadside market and buying a half bushel of marvelous Jonathans. Granny had a frolic making applesauce every day she was with them.

Granny usually carried a big bag which served as purse, correspondence file, repository for schedules, personal effects, and some fetishes, small carvings, etc., that she needed for her exhibits on Haiti. She had been in the States several months and would soon be returning to Haiti. But the bag was worn and mended about as much as it could stand. A friend offered to buy her a new one. "Oh, never. I'll find another at a church sale." Indeed she did, for twenty-five cents. But even it required a little stitching ere she reached Port-au-Prince, its seams threatening to gape open with the ever increasing strain of more added as she headed back toward Miami.

Traveling through the South, Granny found herself on the bus with a church group one day. Two of the women directly behind her were protesting the heavy hand of desegregation. Said one, "You remember that it's un-biblical. God cursed Shem or Bam, or someone. Who was it?" The other lady couldn't remember either, so, having included Granny in the group conversation, leaned over, "You're a missionary. You should know." But Granny was unsure of her own theology on that point, and hardly felt that the topic merited all the fuss. So she took out of her bag some pictures of potbellied, malnourished Haitian children, and began telling her fellow passengers about the plight of the little island ravaged by two recent hurricanes. For the time all was forgotten except Haiti, and before the group got off the bus they took up a collection and gave Granny thirty five dollars.

Another time Granny was traveling by Greyhound and she had to change buses. It was about lunchtime. Her dentures had been bothering her, so she chose a pimiento sandwich and a banana for lunch. She removed her lower plate and enfolded it in her paper napkin and laid it beside the banana peel. A departing bus was announced over the intercom, and, thinking it was her bus, Granny hastily reached for her lunch papers and the peeling, and tossed all in the waste receptacle. Then she gathered up her chattels and started for the bus. "No, Madam, this is not the bus to Miami." Granny then decided she would buy a cup of hot chocolate. When the drink was served, she suddenly realized that her lower plate was missing. She left the counter, retraced her steps, and, lo, the waste disposal had been taken away. In a flurry, she found her way to the kitchen for help. At last she got to the right person, who dispatched two searchers. She waited. The clock moved ahead, unfeelingly. Then over the loudspeaker came, "Bus for Miami now departing." Now certain that her plate had already been consigned to the incinerator, a wilted Granny trundled toward the thrumming bus. At that moment, a janitor, himself disporting only one visible tooth, came triumphantly waving the lost dental plate. His one tooth smiled magnificently alone as he helped a perked up Granny scramble aboard.

As interest in Haiti spread, Granny made friends in a middle course across most of the country. Back at Fermathe, she spent a portion of each day answering her mail. Every letter had to be acknowledged personally. And with each writing she relived the hospitality of now dear friends who were the lifeline of the mission. At Christmas time, she wrote to over six hundred friends.

Now interest was spreading in a broader pattern. A group of churches in Oklahoma would be sponsoring their mission conference early in the year. Could Granny's name be included on the program? Of course she would go. Granny was now eighty five. Other churches would likewise be having mission conferences.

Wallace was helping with her itinerary. But Granny was issuing the instructions on scraps of paper. "Wallace, tell them I want to be kept busy. I'll gladly meet any mission conference of any church or organization, men's or women's clubs, youth groups, children's meetings, or classes in Sunday school, in homes — anywhere — anytime — morning, noon or night, or morning, noon and night. Won't mind two or three meetings a day. I'd like a schedule well filled."

"Each group will see that I get to the next engagement, for I won't know my way around. Long distances I prefer traveling by bus rather than by train... I'll see more of the country, and it's two thirds cheaper. Could go any time in January. I'll stay as long as I'm kept in Oklahoma, Texas, Kansas, anywhere they'd like to hear about Haiti."

"Wallace, I should have a bus clergy for that part of the U.S."

"We have one supporting church in Kansas, at Scott City. And our friends the John Shulers are in Dallas. Maybe they could use me in Dallas and that area. Be good if those states could get interested in Haiti."

"We have plenty of time to think and plan, to get the most out of my going. And we ought to try to reach as many areas in that part of the U.S. as we can."

On this trip to the States, in 1973, a grey haired man came up to Granny in Tulsa, Oklahoma, while she was setting up her display on Haiti, and asked, "Are you Mrs. Holdeman?" "Yes, what's left of her," warmly replied Granny. Then she all but swooned when he told her he was Weaks Martin. He and his wife had driven nine hundred miles just to see her.

Weaks was one of a family of nine boys who grew up in the house next door, when she was doing home mission work in Dover, Tennessee. Forerunner of youth night services, young people would gather one night a week in the young missionary's apartment, make popcorn and candy, talk and sing and have a lot of fun together. Teenage Weaks and one of his brothers came to know the Lord in one of those fellowship gatherings.

He now told Granny of his active church life in Mission, Texas, and took out a handful of sixty year old snapshots of the Dover young crowd and their leader. Their memory feast marked a brief, unforgettable chapter in the lives of both.

Now Granny was speaking daily through the week, and three or four, even six times on Sunday (if someone failed to appear, she took his place too). Anytime she might be heard humming, I'm So Happy in the Service of the King.

Granny would be the first to admit that her humor may not be the latest scream. Yet her zest in telling a whimsical story invariably relaxed and won the confidence of her hearers. Her jests delighted, even the one her Uncle Edras used to tell. "A friend at a barn dance discovered the lace of his partner's petticoat entangled in the buckle of his high top shoe. Being a gentleman, he dropped to his knee and released the ensnared lace. But in doing so, he yielded to temptation and stole a delicious glance at his dancing partner's ankle. And indeed he did the right thing about that indiscretion. He married her!" Granny's chuckle would subside with, "I belong to that era. And, standing here before you I feel about like Bossy. Grazing alongside the highway one morning, Bossy looked up to note the passing of a milk truck that proclaimed, 'Pasteurized Milk, the Safest.' She had hardly resumed her cropping when a second truck went by spreading the word, 'Homogenized Milk, the Best.' Still pondering this one with her cud, a third truck impudently whizzed by, declaring 'Vitaminized Milk, the Healthiest', whereupon an abashed Bossy turned to her companions and said, 'Girls, I feel woefully inadequate'."

On this last trip, her usual suggestion that Haiti can use anything, "your chewing gum and soft drink money, a flounce or ruffle less on your new dress"... sounded a trifle dated. For, even though the Haitians have never put a premium on nudity, they are used to seeing American fashions, and Granny would not admit being shocked if a see-through blouse and shorts should be seen wandering around the mission. She got to the plea this time, then stopped and shook her head. "No, the Haitians should be sending some clothes to American young people!"

As if seeing through a glass darkly, Granny has indicated a reluctance to embark on any more deputation visits to the States. "At my age, if the Lord decided to call me home and I was in the States, it would cost at least three thousand dollars to bury me. If I'm here, Wallace can make my coffin in the cabinet shop and they can bury me in the churchyard for twenty dollars."

However guileless was Granny's reasoning, she didn't get away with grounding herself for long. A church program committee in Texas, bent on making their anniversary celebration special, unanimously named Granny as one of three all time speakers who had meant most to the congregation. They wrote this nonagenarian pilgrim and sojourner on the earth a year ahead. To them she was ageless. And the Lord willing, she went.

Wallace

The young missionary's pabulum
ingenuity matured into a meaty morsel
for his college professor to chew on
with embarrassed incredulity

I f the sky and earth of Fermathe had come to mean home to
Granny more than any place she had ever lived, the mission's
growth force and prime mover was no less than the startling
Midwesterner who became her son-in-law.

In college Wallace's professor would have used the slide rule
and said "Impossible!" to most of the modus operandi of his thirty
years in Haiti. A lean and lank six foot two, built like a college
football player, he bears a good resemblance to a practiced sports
award winner. Because of a relentless drive, the spur that is in his
blood, he seems younger than his fifty some years.

Water Problem

Water was Problem Number One in 1946. It still is.

When the witch doctor abandoned the Fermathe site, the nearest
possible water supply trickled out of the rocks several hundred
feet below into a deep ravine. Drilling was impracticable. Until
something better could be plumbed, gourds balanced on the willing
heads of the women must do.

Mortar mixing for early mission construction moved ahead literally on the heads of women
who brought water a quarter of a mile up the mountain.

Discovery number one was when Wallace burned some of the limestone quarried from the mountainside, slaked it with water, then mixed in some grainy clay, and lo, he had a fine mortar. His discovery was not unlike that of the imperial Romans who found that by mixing a certain kind of earth with calcium hydroxide (limestone and water) they could make a concrete as hard as stone.

Word had come that the rainy season was less than a month away. The young missionary, convinced that every inch of space would be precious, located, gauged, then stepped off four rooms. If the rubble and fill earth could be dumped along the shelf, a few feet could be added outward on the face of the mountain. The foundation could then extend as far as firm rock, and a basement could be dug out later below the shelf.

Organizing the most apt work hands who already had helped make a road and prepare the site, he quickly sketched plans for quarriers, stone cutters, water carriers, and mortar mixers. They had nothing on the Stone Age. Save for an old truck axle or two to pry out the stone, some pieces of scrap metal for chisels and some bent iron for trowels, manpower alone erected their first shelter.

One segment of the labor force hollowed troughs out of the surface and women formed a water gourd brigade to fill them for mixing mortar and concrete. Another muster of women and children scraped up and delivered the rubble and fill earth to the shelf edge of the site, all in baskets on their heads. The quarriers hacked and pried, heaved and hoisted each stone up the side of the mountain, dressed and hauled it into place on the site. A flanking corps crushed limestone by hand for gravel for the concrete mix. The floors would be concrete. The more skilled few helped build the forms, while all the unskilled scooped up the wet concrete and dumped it in the forms. Laying the stones by the simple lintel method, they were zippered or interlocked together for strength. Two or three learned to lay and make level courses of the stone.

Every stone, every gourd, every basket that moved, first had to be hoisted to somebody's head, then carried. Exciting indeed how much a work force can accomplish even under such primitive conditions. Walls fourteen to eighteen inches thick rose with plumbline straightness, cornerstones were shaped and chopped and fitted with surprising niceness. Those walls going up so neatly were the talk of the mountainside.

Haitian helpers work with salvaged corrugated metal roofing for the mission house. All slills are learned ont he job with Pasteur Wallace.

And soon the walls would need a roof, a metal roof. Alas it was the close of World War II. The long list of shortages that plagued people in the States was simply nonexistent on this isle. Nobody was getting metal roofing. Yet, those walls must be roofed. Couldn't friends back in the States help?

Finally, the roofing from a wrecked factory in Philadelphia was on its way to Haiti. But the ship ran into one of those storms that beset the West Indies, and half the precious roofing went overboard; the rest encountered various delays, and the rains started. Still, enough finally arrived on the site in time to shelter the new abode from the spring rains. And there was a new impetus for the work. Eleanor,

Granny's daughter, had come down at Christmastime. From the first, everything pointed to the two becoming colaborers together. Now Eleanor's year of teaching school would end in May, and the two would have a summer wedding.

Safe and dry, Wallace worked inside while the rains pounded the new corrugated metal roof. All that water tumbling off the roof and down the mountainside must be collected and stored for the dry months. An uncommon engineering feat was about to be born. The idea for collecting and storing fresh rainwater, that his prospective bride might have water in the house, could hardly await the rains to cease. The project would require a sure cement.

Summoning the best trained workers, stones again were quarried, dressed and laid in straight courses to form a double row of parallel walls, to become the sides for four tanks. The first would be a settle tank for purification, and from it the overflow would fill the three others. Each tank would have a drain pipe to permit washing and cleaning, and all the tanks would be sealed. Elevation would provide adequate gravity for flow to the kitchen and bathroom plumbing.

At length the four reservoirs were built and plastered at the ends and arched over the top with concrete. It would be weeks before the fall rains would fill them. The Turnbulls, now wed, anxiously awaited the rainy season, each day's supply of water becoming more precious. The women were obliged to drop lower in the ravine each morning to fill their gourds, and each trek back up the steep mountainside took a little longer. Eleanor noted the gourds emerge above the mountain edge and wondered how much longer the supply would last. She found herself uneasily scanning the sky.

There were days of haze, then cloudiness, and then one night darkness covered them like a great velvet wing. Later they were awakened by a tumult of rainwater pummeling the roof and plunging into the new empty reservoirs. After all the weeks and months of quiet, the rain was thunderous. They were closed in by the pounding of rain. The wind blew and thrashed the palmettos, and the rain came in thrusts and gusts for three days. The reservoirs were full. Testing by the health ministry affirmed the water was pure enough to use without boiling or chemical additive. O glorious beginning! These tanks, crude alongside the slimmer later ones of concrete, had set the principle by which water might be conserved and supplied the compound. They were to remain amazingly adequate as the house grew to include office space, more rooms for a growing family and constant guests. And tanks like these were to become part of every roofed unit in the compound. Each new structure was designed to conserve its own roof runoff.

And through the years, essentially the same technology was to serve for Granny's house, the hospital, the nurses' quarters, the guest houses, the church, the TB wards, the pond, walls, driveways and terraces. As cement became available, the reservoirs for all of these buildings could be made larger and sealed to last longer. The essential tools improved somewhat, but no steam shovels or other earth moving equipment replaced human hands and heads. Most of the construction adhered to a simple functional plan, with permanence the primary goal. However, the rainbow dipped again to the mission when Albert Mangones fashioned the tearoom and crafts center with one of his famous stressed concrete roofs. A series of rhythmic rounded shells of concrete, an ectype of the distant mountains, are as much at peace with the setting as the glass and grilles. The same aesthetic touch graces the grilled gate and townhouse façade of the new guest missionaries' apartments.

Withal, the water problem may seem solved, but never is. Hundreds of patients, school children, long and short hostel abiders, others who work or simply come and go—all stand in need of sanitation comfort. The old fashioned outhouse had to suffice, sans much sanitation or comfort, for hostelry and TB wards, until necessity prodded Wallace's engineering talent for another effectual solution.

The TB wards are in fact a camp, a series of units built galleryfashion along the mountain face below the road, the church, and Sunday school rooms. Here patients, with a family member or two, bring along some food and a little burner to cook it, and some bedding. This is home for weeks, sometimes months, until treatment sufficiently arrests the disease so the patient can return to his home. The roofs of these quarters are narrow, only one room wide. When the rains are the heaviest, water cascades from above with such force it wears and cuts trenches into the shelf that serves as walkway and front yard for the units. To reduce the damage, Wallace devised shallow concrete runoffs, then another idea struck: Why not let all this gushing solve the TB camp's human waste problem?

With truck axle crowbars (mountain roads eventually wear out and wreck not a few trucks), a pick, some hand-twisted rope, and a zinc bucket reinforced with the strapping from shipping crates, two veteran workers dug a hole twenty eight feet deep through the rock. By now Wallace had about twenty years of quarrying experience, so he could calculate fairly accurately when and where to begin tunneling in. It took about six weeks and seventy five feet of tunneling from the outside of the mountain inward, to connect with the perpendicular shaft. One hazy day a digger went down and sounded at the bottom of the twenty-eight foot hole. Soon he heard himself answered with a small breakthrough right at his feet. The last few bucketfuls of limestone were hoisted to the top. An underground flume was made ready with some old metal barrels set in cement. The mouth of the hole was fitted with a concrete slab centered with a squatting hole. A three sided wall proclaimed privacy. Each heavy rain flushes the largest flush toilet in the world into the boulders and weeds of the gorge below. So successful was this derring-do, Wallace had another just like it tunneled and poured for the hostel dwellers and mission transients.

Forsooth, success can be claimed, genius of plan and purpose duly acclaimed, and the whole twilight enterprise consigned to the coaction of nature, were it not for the patrons of such noble benefactions. Haitian mountain people, when introduced to the fitness of an outhouse, fail utterly to appreciate the reason for the hole that is there. They eschew it completely. In lieu of the pig staked under the banana tree, a sanitation warden goes twice daily to wash down the outhouse.

Haiti's plains are well watered by rivers, but most of the island is mountainous. Five thousand feet up, streams turn to sandy wastes in the dry season, leaving only a few springs to provide the mountain people with fresh water.

And although these people walk miles for a gourdful of water, they never know the parched agony of those who endure the heat and drought of the desert regions.

Granny remembers the year she lived at seaside Anse Rouge near Atrèl with unforgotten distress. "Your water was thick and black by the time it finally anointed the dirt floor or the few scraggly plants at the door. You had washed yourself, your clothes, and anything else less dirty than the water. Animals never get enough to drink. You feel so sorry for them. But you don't get enough either. The water is brought in gourds that hold three or four quarts. These ride in baskets against the sides of little donkeys from the far ravine. The water may taste of donkey urine since the little animals go in the muck alongside the hole. Only the juice of a lime or sour orange and some brown sugar can mask it. When there are coconuts and sugar cane, you drink the milk of the coconut, peel the cane and give thanks for nature's gratuity.

"The children are so dirty with crud it literally must be scraped off hands and feet. One poor widow with fourteen children would manage a bath of sorts for part of them every fortnight in a halffilled trough hewn out of the trunk of a tree. If the dry season and grippe coincided, there was only the back of the hand, like a windshield wiper, to cope with runny noses."

On the plains the women come to the streams to beat their clothes clean with heavy flat paddles, adding sour oranges for soap and the hot tropical sun for bleach. A mother may bathe her small child or two and herself, then wait about in the cooling water until her dress is dry. Her donkey drinks, she fills her calabashes, collects her small fry and her raiment and begins the climb homeward, lest the fast falling dusk enfold them on the mountain trail.

During the annual three month Bible school, when a hundred or so church leaders come to the mission for instruction and study, Eleanor supervises the laundry for all, to make sure not a drop is wasted. When the pump gives a faint thump thump that announces no more, even if you're all soaped in the shower, the only water is at the spring a thousand feet below. Women and girls will start bringing it up in the morning from the ravine. They fill five gallon cans now and are paid by the canful which rides on their heads on up the steep trail. Usually they make the trip down and up again in forty five minutes; they do this all day long, averaging about ten trips a day.

Only people who have lived both with and without plumbing can appreciate the difficulties of rationed water. But if you are a house guest five thousand feet up in Haiti, you can readily understand, with the rainy season yet weeks away, the sense and sanction of respecting a well posted reminder:

Halt!
Water Shortage Territory

1. Use plug in wash bowl
2. Baths permitted Saturday night only, save only after trip to Nether Regions (Port-au-Prince)
3. Flushing for a wee wee offense absolutely forbidden
4. Flush only for major offenses
5. Please supervise use of water by your household

If, weeks afterward (and you are back in the States), your flushing twinges noticeably lessened, you scan your Newsletter, your relapse may be acute: "Due to the prolonged dry season and a faulty water closet float which went undiscovered in a guest apartment for perhaps two weeks, our water situation has been precarious. Our leaders gather for their annual conference next week. Pray with us for rain."

The Artibonite irrigation program has blessed the plains. But as long as the streams must carry water not only for crops but for washing, bathing, and unhappily, human waste, there will be parasite caused disease. Typhoid and amoebae are spread by fresh water in the rice paddies and canals. Oddly, Haiti is peculiarly blessed and free of one or two tropical infestations. Unlike Puerto Rico and other heavily populated tropical areas, it is the only island not infested with Bilharzia. A few years ago a Harvard scientist studying this fluke (which enters through the soft tissue between the toes and migrates through the bloodstream to the bladder, intestine, liver, and spleen) found that Haiti provides an effective natural enemy. He discovered that a little French horn shaped snail which feeds on the water hyacinths in the Artibonite is also host to a parasite that disposes of the Bilharzia parasite.

Fuel

Wally's methane project might get the slide rule exclusion hands down.

Fuel becomes a more critical problem in Haiti by the day. This paradise of vegetation and timber forests in 1803 when 400,000 slaves seized the land and their independence, has year by year yielded its trees to provide land for crops and to make fuel for a population grown to seven million. To make charcoal for the markets of Port-au-Prince, the Haitian in timbered areas has subsisted by stripping the mountain slopes. He now finds himself to the face of the mountain, his grandfather's small parcel subdivided by a large family and reduced to one tired garden spot which the coming rainy season will erode to the limestone subsurface. Neither he nor any government agency has put a seedling back. His land denuded, defenseless, he is like a squirrel, his one nut tree gone, with a nestful of little ones clattering for food.

To compound the error, the government tax on kerosene, diesel oil, and propane gas places these fuels beyond the reach of the poor. Electricity is not available to 90 percent of the masses. Where starvation and near starvation are becoming the norm, a mother may say, "My children slept without supper. There was food but no fuel to cook it." No cornstalks or dried twigs or dry seed pods, nor even cow dung could be gleaned that day. Too late, government interdiction tries to save the trees that still stand by telling the farmer he can't cut a tree unless it is dead. So he assures its demise by subtly girdling it with his machete, or removing the soil that sustains it.

Even at the mission, fuel is an ever present problem. At first the hospital food was cooked in twenty gallon pots over open wood fires. Wood for even one hot meal a day for 114 patients and dozens of hostel lodgers consumed one sizable log. In time it became impossible to buy a tree, have it cut into firewood and brought over miles of rugged steeps. Scouts searched for dead and dying trees far from Fermathe. Although some propane was used, its cost was too great for cooking; electricity greater.

Wally imported a solar stove from Israel, hoping it could capture enough of the sun's rays to boil the food. Its concentration failed to produce even a simmer. He wrote agencies around the world for methods and devices. Finally, the government of India came through with several forms of generators that could be activated with methane gas.

Methane gas is produced by raw sewage and animal dung, and when ignited the flame is blue, like propane. Although incapable of as many BTU's, it can be designed to raise enough heat for a family size pot. Teaching rural people to develop their own methods of tapping the gas in an inverted dome or tank over a cesspool, or in a closed drum of sewage, then delivering the gas by a metal conduit or tube to the stove, taxes a man's patience more than his genius. As in every innovation to the old pattern of life, there is resistance. On what would the family pig staked to the banana or coffee bole feed if the members stopped squatting before him every morning?

The added bonus of a rapid decomposition thermolysis to produce the methane leaves a safer byproduct for fertilizer than the pig's leavings, for nature will have killed the germs and parasites in the fermentation. It can be compressed and pumped into cylinders and used like propane.

Whenever the Turnbulls left the mission and the island, Wallace forever sought out someone who could help him with Haiti's problems. So it was, on a trip to Mexico, he observed how the Mexican glass manufacturers could, with diesel fuel in their crude furnaces, generate a temperature high enough to melt glass. Why not rig up a diesel burning stove that could cook a fifty gallon pot of food?

He worked out a trestle to support a five gallon can of fuel and erected it six feet above the stove, and from its end he brought some half inch pipe through which he devised a controlled drip by inserting a notched gate valve. This he connected with a horizontal one inch pipe that led into the stove. Every two feet or so, allowance for big cooking pots, he drilled one sixteenth inch openings, two for each pot. Then, a small fire is built with chips and trash each morning to preheat the pipe. As the heated fuel vaporizes, it begins to escape and ignite through these small orifices into a roaring hot flame.

One more challenge on this project: How to find a way to re-burn the exhaust and thus reduce the fuel outgo below the forty cents an hour he now figures it costs to burn the diesel.

They Learn to Make Terraces

All those years before the hurricanes Wallace had preached and practiced reclaiming every foot of wasteland with the stones that cluttered the mountainsides. The rural farmers had politely listened but few had bothered to try Pastor Turnbull's ways, blan ways. Despite the black's proverbial attachment to one who guides and protects him, came the time of moon, and kombit continued to accomplish the traditional routine they had followed for generations, planting their rows up and down, not semicircular as Pastor Turnbull's. Came the hurricanes, and crops, soil and many of their huts moved with the torrents down the mountainsides. Came planting time twice without so much as a little corn or millet or beans blessing their fields with promise. After all those months of suffering, came planting time again. Pastor Turnbull had sent out a call for helpers. Sixteen hundred men showed up, gaunt and ragged. Only two hundred of them could be used at a time for this first demonstration session. Two hundred recruits could return next week, and another group the week following.

Wallace had bought a steep mountainside, eroded, the bare underlayer exposed. With Gerard as foreman, since he had learned to make terraces at the mission, the men first learned to make an A level of three poles in order to follow the curves of the mountainside and to calculate their terrace levels. A team collected stones, another dug trenches, and a third began embedding the base row of stones. Now singing as they worked, a sort of competition emerged as they grasped their task. A second and a third low wall on parallel tiers steadily formed the lower sides of new garden plots. The loosened thin layer was now mixed with whatever debris could be scraped together to make a convincing bed for the precious seed Pastor Turnbull provided.

The next day's team repeated the process on Pierre's garden plot, Jules, the day following. They were turning out in serious enough mood and numbers now to change their feckless ways. No longer as the women cooked the evening meal did the men sit around the small fires and puff cob pipes, talk, brag and bluster that all white men are stupid.

Zafè nèg pa zafè blan. (Blacks and white don't see alike how to do a thing.) How long before there would be mush and beans in the pot? They had nothing, their families were starving.

Pastor Turnbull had initiated a plan the first year of his sojourn with them: the principle of work for benefits—clothing, seed, fertilizer, whatever the mission could offer. The first rooms, the first reservoirs, the first road, had all, and all else afterward, been built on this premise of benefits for on the job training. Even when American donations and surplus food and clothing began arriving for hurricane relief, Wallace held to the rehabilitation and not handout rule. The *idee force* convinced the minister of health, who was in charge of relief, and with whom Wallace worked closely, as well as other government leaders. Demonstrated again and again as relief crews went into the devastated areas with corn meal and beans for those able and willing to work, new character emerged as roads were cleared and bridges built, and hundreds of little huts began reappearing on storm swept sites for the shivering homeless.

Back in the States Senator Dirksen took approving note of his fellow Midwesterner's workable ideas that were literally keeping alive thousands and giving new life to many more. This was in 1960. Spirit touched spirit as the Senator, powerful Senate committee chairman, cited the sense and proof of spending principle that this lone missionary pioneer offered the poorest spot on earth for survival.

Wallace worked with vision. Every project undertaken had to be depended upon to bring lasting benefit to these people.

It was that same year that he constructed a large pond on the wasteland below Granny's house, that it and others like it might provide another protein rich food, fish. The road to the hospital descends sharply to Granny's house. During the rainy season the torrential flow would bite into and even shear off the shoulders of the road. Wallace slanted the road into a side ditch and paved it alongside Granny's house to channel the water, which often brought with it mud and stones. He devised a sump to catch this sediment before it could be carried into the pond. The pond, with four sides of concrete, was seven feet deep at the farthest end. He stocked this large water hole with tilapia, a fast producing fish that thrives in tropical waters and small ponds.

Wally was climbing in the jeep to go up to Fort Jacques where new classrooms were being added to the schoolhouse. "Why not come along? Some pretty good examples of terracing around there.

"We teach them, try to heal them, and lift them from their misery when they come to know the Lord," he was shouting as the jeep left the main road and started climbing straight up a narrow byway. By now the jeep's roupy churning doused all further effort at conversation, so Wallace started singing, choosing to forget our viscera. We braced, then clutched and clung. We rocked and jostled and bounced. We swayed and pitched and lurched. Less than a half hour of this brought us to the hilltop school where several workers were going up with the stone walls. A few yards to the left another group was ready to begin building farmer Titell's terrace. Both groups looked to Pastor Turnbull for their orders for the day.

Down the mountainside as far as one could see, neat, curvilinear low stone walls outlined green and growing garden plots. These terraces for the most part belonged to Haitian Christians. They did not know that Pastor Turnbull's example was teaching them to break their shackles; they only knew that he was their most trustworthy friend. A white man who had in no way gone native, he was more concerned about them than all the socialism schools that came and went. A hardworking man among them, singing, and preaching kindness, taking care of them and now at least succeeding in helping them to a more decent living, he genuinely belonged to them. Even the witch doctors were coming, and once they became Christian, they wanted to help the missionary.

Haitian With His Skin Turned Inside Out

Pastor Turnbull was honest with the Haitians and had no waste space in him. He never traded with them, with God as the middleman. He made no distinction between souls and sores. Both needed healing. Hardier than some who come for a time and then give it up, he had been there longer than any, and unlike most, he could laugh with the people. They said Pastor Wallace was a Haitian with his skin turned inside out. He was a familiar figure laying naked rock, sweating in the sun, a white dark man loved by them, showing them how to rebuild their world. It was all a part of their new religion.

"I wasted a lot on them in the early days. The elements of their early African culture have persisted, even though slavery destroyed much of the old tribal structure as the clan disappeared. Slavery severed all family and tribal identity. They don't live in clans or even in villages. Actually, their villages are cours de famille (family compounds) dotted all over the mountainsides. Of those who are not native, the missionary comes nearest to understanding their ways, and he comes closest to persuading them, after he has managed to quell his own inhibition and bias."

Fort Jacques

Wallace thought that the time lichened ramparts of the brooding old fort, from which the school gets its name, would give a more commanding view of the terraced slopes.

A zigzag road and straining jeep brought us up to this bastion, one of many on the island. The almost vertical slopes were calculated to discourage invasion. The ex-slaves engineered and built this enormous complex of defenses to hold off the French and British besiegers. This was in the early 1800's. Four foot masonry walls lift above sheer cliffs of limestone. That such massive blocks were hewn out of limestone and set in place by sheer human brawn, then long silent cannon hauled and heaved to the upper galleries to command all directions, staggers the mind's eye. No greater wonder are these ramparts than the huge man made reservoir. Wallace saw its vast potential and spent several months with a corps of workers cleaning it out—a tank of stupendous proportions. The smooth upper slopes of the fort only need, even now, a few hundred bags of cement to seal it that it may again collect quantities of fresh water from the rains that lash the island two seasons each year.

As we stood scanning the distance, beyond the northern horizon was the broad Atlantic, to the east Santo Domingo, and across the valley to the south rose lofty La Salle, nine thousand feet high, and the pine forests (Forets des Pins), habitat of the musicien bird and wild strawberries. One day the road will be extended to Jacmel, which is just over the mountain on the map. Closer range took in the expanding pattern of green terracing, the workers at the school, women in their doorways embroidering napkins for the mission outlet shop.

Pastor Wallace and the Haitian Farmer

Wallace was agilely starting the sharp descent back to the jeep, talking. "The Haitian farmer had to see and accept a changed way of life. We showed a group of farmers over the mountain how a pond fed by mountain streams could provide fish for their protein starved children. The idea caught on and they worked awhile, then stopped. Why let others take the fish after we do the work? Now a new generation that can read and write won't continue to be slaves to their superstitions and prey to the unscrupulous. They will have better food, sanitation, and will accept change, spiritual change. When we acknowledge we need the Lord, he changes us. How long before I learned that a few there be that enter means just that!" Then he was remembering Gilbert and Nicolas, and the jeep's motor took over in a daredevil descent to the road.

When we were back at the mission, several awaited direction and help, and a couple of German journalists wanted to talk about the work. Not until the evening meal could he resume.

Wallace began carving the meat. Eleanor picked up the first plate to add portions of rice, beets, and green beans, and observed, "Even though Wally's animal breeding with help from Heifer USA project is now full grown, it's a special treat to have roast beef."

David took up, "Dad sends the bull calves into other areas for up breeding the scrubby island stock. It just takes longer in Haiti, for feeding is half the success. Holsteins are rugged animals that give a lot of milk, but it is hard to find enough to feed them. Pigs and goats we help improve the same way; two or three are counted a herd."

Wallace was reaching for his thoughts.

To help them conquer their backwardness and accept the embrace of civilization depends, as any progress depends, on education. He had known this from the first, when he worked with them with explosive expletives; then he had argued, threatened, cajoled. Only when he took up the pick and calmly showed them, chanting a little work tune in time with his strokes, did they fall in with him. On occasion the dictatorial or pedantic would surface momentarily. But generally this practical idealist, moralist, teacher, humanitarian, scientist, expert in masonry, carpentry, cabinet making, animal husbandry, pharmacy, farming and conservation, was their Pastor Turnbull. Actually, this blan had built houses, church, reservoirs, walls with little more than bare hands—something like making a space trip in a cub flying machine. Although he would like them to work diligently, he accepts facts, and he had accepted the fact that they are Haiti's gift to him. He was here on a mission for the Lord.

With paucity, poverty, and pittance the daily norm in the Haitian farmer's life, his set of values is not the same as yours in an affluent situation. If civilization had washed your shores for two centuries, and you had continued in the indifferent habits of your forebears, who never had to compete for a living, who had a thatch for a shelter, enough food and a loin cloth, you too might be dancing and singing in "freedom", unaware and uncaring that the mercilessly tightening bondage of your own ignorance was eclipsing your island home in sinister darkness.

As Wally talks about the Haitian, you are sure he has walked in his sandals. "The rural farmer may be robbed of food, but never his easygoing nature. He strides along the mountain roads and yells Bonjou to every one he meets. He dances and invents rhythms and he lets his emotions sway all his choices and decisions. All his work is done with much singing and jesting, and he cherishes any fellow who can make him laugh. Immune to scolding, he feigns deafness and looks away; sarcasm is every bit wasted on him. He will agree with whatever you ask of him with an expressionless face, and likely as not promptly forget.

"Machinery fascinates him, but he treats it as a toy. The parts of a clock enchant him, but never expect him to put them back to work. It's not easy to appraise his lack of feeling for driving a nail straight, or finishing a board with the grain. He will burn a plank of taverneau for firewood. He will take the food of a patient at the hospital. Time means nothing to him; if he doesn't get there when the service begins, there will be many more like him. If his goat eats your happily maturing garden, he will not be around to claim him. But if you run over his goat, he's there for a claim on the spot.

"His politeness is remarkable. One ragged farmer addresses another as monsieur and madame. If you see boorishness and curtness, it is the urban Haitian, whose manners don't always equal those of the rural people. And you can never be sure how to regard his honesty. Even the bank clerk has trouble distinguishing between mine and thine. Present your teller, as we did, a handful of checks amounting to around $600.00. Explain that you wish $465.00 in cash for hurricane relief work, and the remaining $135.00 left on deposit. See him, like Henny Penny in a flurry of alarm, counsel with first one then another of the tellers and cashiers and finally a director. In their deliberate and corporate wisdom they decide that maybe the sky is not falling in. So with a smile and a swagger, but no apology for the two hour wait in which young Sandy has broken away whooping wild, we are on our last legs, and Granny and David have sweltered in the jeep, the young banker pushes through the money and slips.

Growing Leaders

"It was ten years before we had the first three month Leaders Institute—ten years growing some. Bringing them together in this work study, their lives are changed. Although Bible study and church ministry are basic, they learn elementary hygiene, growing and preparing food, building a shelter, using simple tools, animal husbandry, making a home, and something about the rest of the world. A map of the world is sure to evoke incredulity. All are eager to learn. To some who have learned to read, marvels are opening up to them. And we marvel at the good these institutes have wrought. Nights grow chill and even the draperies come down to make cover for those sleeping on mats in the basements."

By far, Wallace's most important assistance to Haiti might be through these leaders, for they come from more than 70 churches and 68 outstations, to which they return and lead over 70,000 growing Christians toward a life more abundant. Sixteen ordained pastors know French in order to comply with government requirements in making out marriage certificates or other legal services. Each pastor is responsible for ten to twelve churches. When forty believers meet in a hut or under a brush arbor, they constitute a new church group. The kids come to the same place for school. They learn while balancing on poles for benches. Although a blackboard and chalk are fairly standard equipment, it is not uncommon to see practice sessions taking place with sticks and sharp stones on the ground.

Eleanor took up the conversation. "The youth camp site had belonged to the mission for several years, but we had not managed to build. Only a stone's throw from the President's beach residence, it obviously might be coveted. Building on a site proves ownership. Neighbors had been harassing government officials to confiscate and resell the plot of land. Granny saved the site when her visit in the States, a few years ago, was cut short by the discovery of a lump in her breast. Friends started sending money to help on what they knew might be an expensive hospitalization. Having often been heard to say, 'Bury me where I fall,' she now grew a little fearful that her feet might be a trifle unsteady, so she hied herself back to Haiti for her surgery.

And saved enough to haul the youth camp fund out of the red and pour footings for the first building on the site. (It was a benign tumor.)

Dieula had taken away the plates and returned with the coffee. As Eleanor began pouring the fragrant brew, for a moment no one spoke. Through the open windows a distant faint sound punctured the night. All at the table heard it — the beginning beat of a Voodoo drum.

Voodoo

How to deal with their charms and fetishes and curses, tokens of their bondage to the real world of spirits..."It filled my days and haunted my nights," Wallace took up again. "It is not bad luck that the branch of the tree breaks and a man is killed, or that he gets skin disease and his neighbor does not. Some evil has wished it upon him. Jon dies because a child puts a harmless bean in his ear while he sleeps. Charms and curses work by the power of suggestion. It had been suggested to him weeks before.

"Every household has its medicinal plants, its sacred tree and fetishes. The dead members of the family are now spirits captured and set to work by sorcerers or deities. These spiritual beings (loas) share the peasant's virtues and failings and, like him, must depend upon a supreme being who is unfeeling toward human affairs. Since this supreme god (Bon Dieu) is indifferent to his supplication, Voodoo is directed almost solely to the loas, these intermediate beings who keep in perpetual contact with the world of men. Because they are unpredictable, impish, capricious, cruel and dangerous, and revenge the people with misfortunes, they must be placated and appeased. And they are a whole pantheon. Le Bon

71

Dieu does not cancel out Damballah (lawmaker) or Erzulie, queen of love, or Ague (navigator), Oueddo, or other deities who by whim can blight your corn or save it, burden you with ulcers or cure an ugly burn, deal you the jack of spades and send a dead soul from the cemetery to plague you, or worse, drop you the king of hearts and dispatch a few devils to take over your household. You are all set to buy a goat, but your outlay for food and drink and perfume to please the spirits took it all. One was not pleased, so you bought candles and mirrors to aid him in seeing how to help you, or as a last resort, you bought some chain and a sword to fix him while you call upon him in a ceremony at which your neighbors and friends sample your last chicken. What's more, in all this you can't snub your witch doctor. He's your medicine man. He's usually the most intelligent man on your side of the mountain and you need him to exercise a charm to ward off the fevers that took two of your children. You also need him to explain that paraffin candle curse at your door (which usually means that you'll never finish your house). But if you are plagued with venereal disease, here your medicine man is most liable to run out of soap. This common affliction taxes him the most. Your neighbor Paulgene came to the mission for the magic needle and he got well. So you come.

You can get only one dose of terramycin if you have a fever too, for if the doctor trusts you with a week's supply to get you back on your feet, you'll surely sell some of it in order to pay the witch doctor for his remedies."

"He comes also to escape his religion's impossible demands," added Wally "He sees the Christian's lot improve. The Christian learns to be more prudent and sensible; he also has a peace of mind, that deliverance from fear that the Voodooist can never know.

"He will come asking to be converted, hoping the white man will give him medical care and a job, but not with the idea of giving up the ritual that has been a part of every moment of his life, but in some way of availing himself of a greater charm. Yon jou pou dyab, you jou pou Bondye (A time for the devil and a time for the Good Lord)."

Wally took up, "We seldom pray with the Haitian in his final decision for Christ. Local Christians pray with him. He then waits a year for baptism, meanwhile attending a weekly class to learn the Christian way. At the year's end he is examined by the church before he is accepted. Most of those who are baptized become active workers in the church and witness to their relatives. It sometimes takes years to bring a relative. Some fear to be saved lest their patron god or dead relative may in fury destroy them while they are making the changeover."

How much does he understand his involvement with the devil?

Practitioners of black magic usually admit openly that they have made a pact with the devil. They can actually produce spells that bring illness or death. Cows go dry mysteriously, animals die unaccountably. A practitioner can do awesome things. There is no naturalistic explanation. Satan and evil spirits actually are responsible. Human beings who establish a mystical relationship with Satan are given power over all the people they encounter. Power is the ultimate lust for which most will sell their souls.

The people's contact with the spirit world is through his witch doctor as a medium. His bocor enters a trance in order to receive the communication. Then whatever vision appears to him or whatever words he utters constitutes the prophecy. The trance has provided entrance for demonic powers when subconscious forces are removed from conscious control.

Not a few come to Haiti to learn that the Haitian people's ignorance and superstition make a poor field for a summer missions walkaway. After the Haitian comes to trust you beyond your novelty value, which is considerable, maybe years later he will become a believer. He will have prayed and lived his Scripture passages such as I John 4:4—Greater is he that is within you than he that is in the world, and become satisfied that Satan is unable to harm him. And though Satan claims that he is prince of this world, and quite possibly headquarters here, he trembles at the light of a truly godly person. Granny sees to it that the new believer's breastplate of righteousness attests some rigorous memorizing of

Scripture. Who can doubt the genuineness of his faith when he recites with face aglow on Sunday morning John 3:16, John 14:15, II Cor. 5:21?

Does this fresh outbreak of the demonic in the States relate?

Antiquity claimed that bodily illness was due to demonic influences. The Middle Ages blamed psychic disturbance on demons. Modern scientific conception denied demonic possession until civilization's burgeoning drug culture brought on a field day in mood and mind changing—with accidental death, suicide, rebellion—and a frank admission that excursion into the psychic phenomena exposes one to a very real danger. The spiritual is not explained away in physical terms, but the view holds that contact with the active malicious spirit world may allow a transcendent power such as a supernatural being operate in a person's life.

Wally, explained, "Our friend Father Jobe avers that no Catholic priest has been able to wean the Haitian from his ancient gods."

"It takes time," Wallace resumed. "Voodoo is African-Latin here. The predominant beliefs and superstitions are Guinea. The practices are Congo. Damballah and his consort Oueddo are considered ancestors of the human race. The green snake is the symbol of Damballah, and in primitive analogy they equate it with the lamb which is the symbol of Christ. Their celebration days coincide with Catholic saints', days, hence the appearance of Mary and the saints in Voodoo temples. And all of these are predominantly good spirits. Congo rites believe in evil ones, requiring bloody sacrifice. Blood sacrifice that includes human beings has always been an integral part of primitive religions. In Haiti, followers of Voodoo believe that certain qualities dwell in the bodies of the dead and when eaten these qualities are absorbed—the heart for courage, the liver for cunning and immunity to edged weapons, the brain for unerring aim.

"Priestly function is handed down from father to son. While a sacrifice is made to honor a god, it also conciliates the inferior or malevolent spirit, Satan. During a ceremony of impassioned drumming and incantation, the bocor (priest) offers a prayer and sacrifices a cock by biting off its head. He smears the blood over the faces of the worshipers and drinks some of it. A goat may be sacrificed and, after that, one of the sorcerers may wish a goat without horns (a child) be sacrificed. Dominated by emotion and the melancholy rhythm, the members of the cult actually are moved by mysterious forces, to them supernatural beings, that control and direct their lives. Since occasional human sacrifice is offered from within the group, all having taken the oath of secrecy, ritual cannibalism of this sort never reaches public notice. Yet strange things happen everywhere. Among people given to orgies, mysticism, and ceremonies, they seem more especially to happen in Haiti.

"Take possession. It is the central feature of Voodooism. Most serious illness is believed due to possession by evil spirits. These must be forced out by good loas. When the loa mounts the person possessed, he replaces that person's soul, and all thought and behavior thereafter are attributed to the loa. In order to explain it, combine the intense drum rhythm with rum and fatigue and various emotions—anger, fear, exaltation—and the higher function of the central nervous system is broken down. After rum and dancing in a rolling, shaking, shocking manner has ripened the mood, there is a sudden shriek and a woman casts herself in the open hounfor. Presently another follows suit, and another, and the drums change beat. There is leaping, whirling, and wild shouts. All become participants, chanting antiphonally, the papaloi providing the lines. The gods are besought to spare their crops, spare their homes, spare their children, spare their donkey and goat, spare their fighting cock, their calabashes and their other worldly goods. Hysteria for some now becomes a socially acceptable guilt reducing device. The depressed, those given to neurotic tendencies, and who can say that all are not, there is the communal couch on which the participant may be restored by a naturalistic psychotherapy. Some may be cured of other maladies of the flesh. A girl suffering from brain fever may be treated with poultices of soap suds and leaves from the bois cochon tree, with incantations and gashes in the scalp, and still recover. It's truth and superstition walking side by side. But the Christian believer is taught that possession is of the devil, and no longer can an evil spirit possess him. Tempt him perhaps but, as a child of God, he is kept from the power of evil.

"Take sorcery. It is no fallacy that the witch doctor can kill without recourse to poison, accident or violence, although he may be adept with all of these. He believes profoundly in the supernatural himself. Black magic is the reverse of mental therapy. It is induced autosuggestion. The doomed victim knows and fears. With the ominous beat of the drums he can literally be hounded by emotion and mind to death. Magic, as we think of it, is trickery or sleight of hand. To the Haitian it is vital. He depends on it to cope with the terrors that lurk about him. It is black magic when it kills. It is white magic when it saves. To his primitive mind this is science. The American black puts a piece of copper in a wound. (Copper sulphate is antiseptic.) The leaf doctor who practices herbal medicine may use green squash (cooling to the blood), red squash (warming to the blood), juice of the sour orange and chicken gall (containing tannin) for dysentery, a plaster of hot cornmeal and leaves of aconite or belladonna to soothe a sprained foot. A cure with what seems to be magic is fruit off the same vine.

"Take black magic. Demonism. A bocor picks up a red hot bar and capers violently with it between his teeth during a ceremony. Outsiders see this act and cry trickery. But testimonials of witnesses whose reach of mind cannot be denied are abundant. Satan is no shrinking violet in disporting his talents. He chortles with exhibitionism. A well known practitioner stopped at a restaurant, tossing his canny baton to the edge of the roof as he entered. The rod impishly began spinning and continued to spin all the time the bocor was inside.

"The police were called repeatedly to halt the thievery of a store. Search of the building after each offense uncovered no disturbance of locked door or windows. At length a suspect was arraigned with recently taken goods from the store in his possession. Returning to the spot with the police, the culprit reenacted his spirit over matter entry through a three inch drain pipe—and reappeared before their eyes with a carton of canned goods under his arm.

"To dance on fire, eat glass, wash the face in burning brandy, brandish the machete, all with no untoward effect, are common aspects of demon presence, supernatural demonstrations that many outsiders have witnessed.

"Leogane, on the south coast, is old stomping ground for witch doctors. They gather there annually to compare practices, and some go back to Africa to learn anew.

"Our secretary tells the story of a prospering young Syrian, whom we shall call Paul, who asked his Haitian friend Pierre to accompany him into the northwest above St. Marc. When the two arrived at their secluded destination, they found themselves among well dressed men partaking of a banquet, a portion of which obviously was a human sacrifice. Out of mortal fear for his life if he refused, the Haitian downed a portion when it was offered him. His Syrian host had joined a serious group aside in conference. At length he returned, handed Pierre the keys to his car and spoke tersely, 'Take the car and all you find in it. Go!' Pierre obeyed, numb with terror. When he reached the Syrian's home in Port-au-Prince and told the story to his mother, she listened emotionless. She knew that her son was a doomed victim. She also told Pierre to take the car. When he opened the trunk, he found a large sum of money which Paul had hoped in vain to be his ransom.

"A little eight year old girl disappeared from Port-au-Prince. The mother besought the police, who shrugged her off. Later, several children under twelve years of age (goats without horns) were discovered held in a remote confine above Leogane. The keepers, unwilling to resist the police, let them go, and escaped charges.

"Black magic involves the direct solicitation and help of demons. White magic, no less the devil, is Satan masquerading as an angel of light using God's name.

"Witchcraft, embraced by the hippie culture the past decade, is actually making a pact with Satan in exchange for magical powers. But one can also look in high places. Imagine men in politics, key men in government, possessed of such power. Imagine them able to reward and deprive, enrage and pacify, favor first one side, then the other, and still keep control. Imagine men of finance working in such power in tandem with the politician and the industrialist. Imagine a people enslaved by their leaders who keep them in ignorance and poverty and superstition. Who else would be so hell-bent on helping man destroy himself, only Satan!

"Take charms and fetishes. Charms that influence the spirits are:

1. Food, drink, scented soap, flowers etc. to please the loa.
2. Candles, tapers, lamps, binoculars, mirrors, symbolically to light the way for favors requested.
3. Nails, pins, needles, thread wire, ropes, locks, keys, vines to bind to fulfill obligation. A sword or bayonet or piece of iron stuck in the ground fixes the attention of a spirit during a ceremony.
4. Sometimes a rural person will wear a garment of a certain color in penance to appease an offended spirit until the garment rots to nothingness.
5. Fetishes include three dimensional wooden or pottery bowls in which all the gods, divided into three groups reminiscent of the Trinity are fed. Three pebbles house a god.

"The cross, the star, and other Christian symbols, bowing, kissing the altar, sprinkling water, lighting candles, and being blessed by the priest all relate to the Catholic ritual, borrowed by the slaves from their Catholic owners to enhance their ceremonies.

"At your door, the cross means a curse; your house will be sold to Baron Samedi of the cemetery.

"A bit of paraffin at your door will condemn you to work on your house without end. Crossed nails forewarn of illness, maybe death. And pins curse you too. Ersulie's spirit will pierce your heart.

"You may wear a black stone as Gede's charm; a white one, Ersulie's. You are pleasing Damballah if your undershirt is maroon; Ersulie if it's yellow; Bologni if it's white; Ogon if it's green. Your necklace will be yellow beads if Damballah dictates your choice; red, white and black if it's Gede.

"You read the cards. The king of spades may let you get sick but it will also get you well; not so the queen of spades. You will not recover, for Baron Samedi asks food in the cemetery.

"The jack of spades imparts a foreboding. The man you are in dispute with may send a dead soul from the cemetery to plague you.

"Beware of the ten-spot. Baron Samedi of the cemetery calls for you. If you have the nine, and you're sick, you won't rise.

"But draw the eight and perhaps you will.

"With hearts and clubs and diamonds you might fare a little better, but the best you can get away with is the eight of clubs, when Ersulie will be asking for your patched undershirt."

"And we have had our share of curses," Eleanor recalled. "When TiWally was four years old, the witch doctor said that he would die within the year. The witch doctor died that year...

"The doors and windows at first were all fastened with big iron hooks. One morning Wallace opened the front door to find a handful of fetishes — some black thread, safety pins, wax paper, and a small cross. That night the hook fell."

Back Country

That was when syphilis ran forty percent, malaria twenty percent, and yaws higher than fifty percent of the population. The common killers were dysentery, nephritis, diarrhea and TB, and we had only one hospital bed per three thousand population. A grass covered arbor in Granny's yard, fenced closely with poles, was the dispensary.

"Anyone who wants to round out his education completely should come with us on one of these back country treks." Eleanor was leafing through notes made on her first of such trips in the summer of 1949.

In the Remote Districts

In the northwest we had arranged five day gatherings in the outlying districts far from hospital or doctor to hold clinic—clear up their yaws and ulcers and give injections. We would meet daily with the earliest workers, visit some church members, pay salaries, if fifty cents to a dollar could be called a salary, and distribute school supplies. These unimpressive groups who assembled under the open thatches hardly bespoke promise, but in these groups were early converts with little education but much enthusiasm for the spread of their new faith.

TiWally was six weeks old. Since the country Wallace was going to visit was above Anse Rouge where Granny had spent more than a year, I decided to take the baby and go with him by jeep. We would travel some of the roughest terrain, over mountains, through gorges, making our own road up dried up river beds, down ravines.

No one who ever took this trip would judge me guilty of hyperbole. I would clutch and hold on for dear life with TiWally; Wallace would calm me with, 'Oh, this is not so bad. Wait until we turn off the road.' What road? At times the only ruts were the jeep tracks made months before on Wallace's first trip through this hot, dry region. Inland from the coast, only cacti and mesquite offered any hint of green. No rain had fallen up here in two years. Our goal lay beyond this scanty waste past where the dry bed of the river led to an area as remote and little known as any on the island—where the heat spikes your mind and stifles your will and man and beast sizzle under the sun.

We sweltered in a slime of late afternoon torridness as we turned to follow the sea the last few miles. A harsh wind swept over the sere land, parching our lips, our eyes rimmed with the limestone dust surging in our wake. As night fell, what passed for our road, furrowed and pitted and overgrown with stubborn shrub, became even more teeth-shattering. Two hours or more of this brought us to Anse Rouge. Grateful at last for absence of motion, I got out, leaned against the jeep, searched my baby's tiny face, and thanked God for the prospect of rest.

The hut which was to be our shelter was sweltering hot. The only opening besides the door was closed with a shutter of sorts. Too exhausted to lend Wallace a helping hand with unloading our canvas cots and bedding, I bestirred myself to let in a little more air. My effort in the dim light disturbed a scorpion that swiftly discharged his resentment in my left forearm. Among all those firsts, that scorpion sting eclipsed heat and cactus and mesquite and tortuous roughness. Since then I learned to avoid this bane, although many times he lurked in the rafters, sluggish in the daytime but out at night likely to be underfoot if we stepped out of bed without first making a light. Ranging from one to three inches in length, the scorpion is a near relative of the spider. He carries a curved needle at the end of his tail through which he delivers a paralyzing sting. His thrust is formidable, sufficient to kill small creatures and even a human being in weakened state.

Washing by the sea in the moonlight and a few hours sleep, and fresh fish for breakfast fortified us for another day over makeshift bridges, across deep ravines and through the trackless back country, encouraging converts like Sada. Sada walked miles to work in the salt mines. Her legs and arms scarred by the sharp crystals, her meager wages scarcely enough to pay forty cents a month for a room and her mush and beans, still she sang praises to the Lord and spread joy as she worked.

By sailboat from Anse Rouge to Baie de Henne—by night because no wind favored us earlier—we endured a rough sea, with water splashing over the sides of our leaky fifteen foot boat until we came to land again in the early dawn. Stationing our men along the way to thwart thieving, we passed our baggage in and set up our cots in an old tumbledown house. The roosters were crowing, although it was only a little past midnight. In the ceiling of that grotesque old house, years of animal deposits—rats and bats—stifled our scant sleep with musty closeness then daybreak brought a delirious razzia of flies swarming over us.

We rented a three room house that day from the judge. It took scraping and sweeping and washing before we could set up our cots, a table, a box for a cupboard, some worm-eaten chairs, and a barrel for water in the corner. Clouds of flies had preceded us. Nothing could be done without shooing the oft-coming dark swarms. We cooked mostly on a small outside charcoal fire. Three times a day I squatted Haitian style over that fire to cook our rice. A chicken, fish, and a goat augmented our menu with a few eggs for which the children asked one cent each. Pigs, goats, dogs invaded our yard—and the house if we failed to bar it against them—to devour the waste; that is until old crippled Luc the beggar came. He staved them off that he might eat the peelings, fish heads, raw chicken entrails before we could stop him. He continued doing this even after we had given him food. Meristen, one of the evangelists with us, protested "Pastor you taught us that we should take care or disease will kill. Luc denies it."

Our effort for Bible school brought meager returns. The children did not come. One small tyke echoed the mind of his heathen parents, "If I go I might get the mind to enter the Baptists." Nonetheless, the two weeks showed an average of twenty three who did come. The dispensary made a better showing. We pulled teeth with workshop pliers. We stitched a twelve inch gash which a man suffered hauling a log for a mast pole. After several miles astride a donkey in the heat, and weak from loss of blood, he gritted his teeth and clenched his fists while we worked with needle and thread. Another man was brought to us on a straw mat his body covered with ashes apparently moribund. As I searched for his pulse, he died. The sudden stridor that broke forth from those standing around stopped my pulse for a startled moment. I was to learn that the shrieks, chants, surging outcries, and jerking motions were not from grief for the departed one, but to fend off evil spirits and to convince the dead not to haunt the living.

It was a little girl, unconscious two days with a fever who made us feel like Elijah on Mount Carmel. We talked with some of the heathen family, explained how God's power can prevail in answer to prayer. We prayed and God heard. By the next morning the fever had gone. She awoke and took food and soon was well. It's God's way to grant miracles to missionaries now and then—for ourselves as much as for the Haitians.

TiWally fascinated the natives. He was the first white baby most of them had ever seen. They would peep in the window stand in the doorway and wait for hours for us to bring him out. When he became ill they brought leaves and plants from which I should make a healing tea. One mother insisted that I make a poultice of ear wax and my milk and tie it over his navel. But he grew worse and it was agreed that I should take him back to Port-au-Prince to a doctor. I left in a fifteen foot boat with seven natives the afternoon sun burning down on us and the azure sea.

We tied up at Gonaïves after the last camion so we were there overnight. The next day was an eight hour trip by camion. People on top were packed as closely together as those inside all with loads of baggage varying from chickens to calabashes. Everybody and everything became covered with a thick film of dust which nobody seemed to mind. The wayfarers laughed and joked together and ate sugarcane and pistachio nuts. Stops accommodated every passenger's whim be it to buy coconut juice to drink or to find a tree afterward (no wayside stations in Haiti).

After two days and one night of this we arrived in Port-au-Prince dirty and weary worn castaways. We found water to clean up, then a doctor. We arranged to stay in Petionville so the doctor could see the baby daily and he improved rapidly. Back in Fermathe, TiWally adjusted again to his outgrown basket on the stone ledge while I helped Granny see 535 patients at the dispensary and portioned out worm medicine to ninety seven more. The day following I set out over roads and trails now slick from heavy rains to visit our sick Christians.

"Making back country trips in later years became hardly less an endurance test, but the rewards were greater. The work was growing. Visits to the desert regions still demand hardihood to bump over trackless terrain, then over barren stretches of lowland where the limestone becomes so finely pulverized a thick white cloud swirls in the jeep's wake. And if someone is ahead, we eat his dust for miles before we can pass. Finally, resembling scarecrows dragged through a limestone quarry, we arrive parched and exhausted, but at once surrounded by friends embracing us in welcome. And eager to share their news and needs.

"Some are sick. Some relate the rude news of vandalism of church property, or that Jacque's wife had taken up with Jerome. Or Zeke's daughter was burned in a Voodoo ceremony—they didn't count on dropping her when the hougans passed her over the fire. Or Tiandre has been taken by a carnival group, and his mother has left on a donkey to find him.

"There was Vierge (Virgin)—what were we to advise her to do? The mother of eleven children, the youngest only two years old, she had become a Christian several years ago. The church advised her to leave her 'unsaved' husband unless he agreed to marry her and leave a second more recent concubine. She felt she could not. Then she had only eight children and was working hard carrying sand, stone and water to build their house. Her man had promised her he would marry her when he could. She had to remain in the believers class and could not transfer to regular Sunday school because she could not be accepted for baptism until she was married. (I wonder before God if she has not been married to him all the time.) The eldest daughter has TB and the mother was begging for medicine, a warm sweater, a little flour to make some pudding. The children were hungry. Four of the children should have been in school but the father would pay the twenty cents for only one. Worn, tired, thin, Vierge reached trembling arms toward heaven, praying: 'To you, God, who created me, and you, Blessed Jesus, who saved me and turned my thinking around, if it please you, take me home to heaven.' Weeping inside, I tried to tell her that she had disobeyed God when she continued to live with this man not married to him. And I wondered if what I was saying was true!

"There was Tibo. He borrowed a dollar to pay a man to take him to the hospital in Port-au-Prince where his three year old child was almost blind from malnutrition. The nurse told him he must give the child food that he did not have.

"But you have ripe banana? 'Yes, but we sell them green for boiling. Ripe banana will rot the teeth. I don't give him ripe banana.'

"Why don't you milk your goat and give the milk to your child? 'If my neighbors pass and see me milking the goat, they will call me poor man...' After spending the night he will walk nine hours tomorrow back to his home.

"There was Catule who brought a Christian woman whose house had burned. Fortunate that the five children and she got out, but they now had nothing... The clothing we gave will help, but not enough.

"There were Juser and Saul incurring a big debt having an expensive coffin made for their father, not yet dead. And the widow will have nothing.

"There was Maizie. Her ragged dress tied together indicated she had no needle and thread. But it was clean, evidence that she was a Christian. Her eyes downcast, she began, 'Madame, you know I never come to ask, but God showed me in my prayers to come. Since two days we've not lifted the pot onto the three rocks where we cook.' She had five little ones, a husband in bed for seven months with glandular TB. She had buried a twelve year old son a few months ago, vomiting blood, and only now had found courage to come for help for her husband. She had nothing to sell to buy medicine. We gave her cornmeal, flour, beans and lard to last a few days. What then?"

The Mountain Flocks

"Visiting the mountain folk is less exhausting emotionally. We find them more kind to one another. They work harder for less, and they can accept the Christian ethic more convincingly. The lowlands seem to breed a lower caste. The youth are less pliable, quicker to cheat, tougher, as are urban youth all over the world."

The trip up to Furcy never fails to exhilarate. After miles of unbelievably deep and boulder strewn ruts, through which the jeep strains and cavorts, we emerge from a seemingly uninhabited wilderness of mountain pines to a scant clearing. Furcy is like an Alpine village in a wild and sadly beautiful region. In the yard of a cliff side house a cascade of bougainvillea plunges down the steep mountainside. Farther down, a few stalks of corn tassel in scrawny deceptiveness. Straight down the side, so steep a Haitian goat or burro might search for his foothold, farmers scratch the soil and plant millet and potatoes. In the soft silence, one may hope to hear the exquisite flutelike notes of the oiseau musicien, an almost extinct songbird heard in these remote cathedral twilight pine forests.

Nearby, in this highest elevation of any flock on the island, are many of the most zealous. What one does hear is the falsetto notes of What a Friend We Have in Jesus, or the weird high-pitched, wailing refrain of a Negro ballad.

Another remote section, where strangers were not known until a few years ago, is Nouvelle Touraine. This was a first trip account from Eleanor's diary:

To bed at midnight, up at 2:30 to leave for Nouvelle Touraine. Drs. Wiss and Sterlin went with us. My horse lay down six times and Wallace's bucked and pranced so much he gave up riding and walked. When we reached the village about ten o'clock, several hundred had gathered with all their ills.

Too tired to reckon how many doses of worm medicine I fixed or how many syringes I filled for the magic needle (VD) we turned over a piece of a banana leaf lest it had served as a chicken roost and ate from our host's cooking pot. We know we helped, especially the babies and young children covered with yellow pustules of yaws. Some were so weak and ravaged by the disease relatives brought them on their backs or in swings of old sacks. We could do little for the advanced TB patients. TB wears an even worse stigma in these isolated areas.

The two doctors took the cots and slept in the chapel.

Wallace and I had only two hand hewn boards. People began gathering about five thirty the next morning for the needle and medicine. The doctors worked steadily until twelve thirty, ate a little food, then left Wallace and me to finish with the patients and teach a class to the children.

The little chapel of palmiste boards with a tin roof has only a dirt floor, on which most everybody sits. We are sure there are fleas, too. This little enclosure serves as dispensary and chapel and hostel for us. Some of the people have chairs, others improvise with hand hewn boards. Stiff and aching from our climb and our first night on boards we had a night service and showed some pictures which they thought were zombies (ghosts). And because there was no moon about 300 stayed until daybreak the night splintered for us by their talk and the beat of the drums across the valley. Sheer exhaustion finally let us claim a little sleep.

Not what we did but what one of our most zealous workers did later changed that remote mountain area.

Victor Felix, born in the rural mountains, had gone to school in the city, learned to read and write, led a Rara band, peddled bread for awhile, and, at length, returned to his mountain farm home where he came under the influence of Granny's and Wallace's teaching and became an ardent Christian worker. Victor went to the Nouvelle Touraine area and began such a remarkable campaign of witnessing, over 500 believers have turned in their fetishes and medicine bottles and turned to the Way.

It was Victor who told us about a witch hunt. An epidemic had claimed a number of the children in a cours famille. Sene Victor's uncle was the family witch doctor. He called a feasting ceremony in honor of the family's patron god Petro. Petro was a fierce god who formerly demanded a goat without horns (child) sacrifice, but now is appeased with a pig.

Members of the clan dared not be absent from the gathering, for fear of death within three months. Some worked feverishly to earn enough to buy food. Others fattened their pig, chickens, or goat. Some readied the set of drums cleaned up and erected an arbor in front of the Voodoo temple hut. On the day of the event, chickens, pigs, and goats were killed in ceremonial fashion, cooked in round bottom pots with much rice and cornmeal and tubers. Sene traced the Petro vever in cornmeal on the ground in a perfect ritual while various family members sang, then danced to the increasing rhythm of the drums, and waited possession by Petro. At length

Victor's mother shrieked and fell into a frenzy. The men tied her in a chair and Sene, flogged her with a congo bean limb until Petro became docile and accepted food. After ingesting a great quantity of food, he divulged that the witch was an unpopular old aunt. Two of her nephews were delegated to strangle her.

Foibles, Fete, and Fellowship at Fermathe

The rural Haitian girl, as a rule, is not expected to know more than how to work in the garden, wash the clothes, and cook the food, all in a simple, primitive fashion.

"What we lacked in conveniences, and there were hardly any, our Haitian neighbors made up in helping us," Eleanor was saying as Dieula took away the plates and brought in a luscious orange red mango dessert.

Although Granny denied being impatient with help in the kitchen, there soon had to be a girl learning their way of cooking, one to wash, one for the house, and a boy for outside the house, and, as the compound grew, any number of hangers-on eager to work for a little money. Granny considered such a retinue more of an annoyance than a help, since one and all plagued for pay, and their irresponsibility could wear even saintly patience thin. The educated and most of the foreigners who come to the island have servants, specifically a cook, a laundress, a housekeeper, and a yard boy, for they persist in doing one thing only. The cook has a full job if she saves the lady of the house from going to market. And the yard boy washes the car and jeep and cuts the grass and disposes of the trash. He may also sweep.

Eleanor takes the girls and trains them to do housework; they can then earn twenty dollars a month in the homes of the educated, the diplomats and foreign business people.

The Girl in the Mission Kitchen

Dieula was beginning her training in the kitchen. Eleanor showed her how to wash the dishes. First in warm soapy water, then rinsing, then scalding. Eleanor came back awhile later and found her squatting, dishpans and dishes, all on the floor, carrying out the ritual just as she had been told. On the floor was the only way she had ever known.

Amancia was helping get dinner for visitors whom Wallace was bringing from the airport. An evening chill had settled and Eleanor thought a little fire in the fireplace would dispel the coolness and add warmth and cheer to the welcome. She told Amancia to build a small fire in the living room. A few minutes later she came in to find smoke filling the room. Amancia had built a small fire in the wood box beside the fireplace.

Before the mission had the luxury of electricity, the pride of the Turnbull household was an Aladdin lamp. The brightness of this lamp resided in the fragile "mantle" which was woven of asbestos saturated in plastic glue. When the glue was burned away the fabric which remained glowed with a white bright light. This filament became incandescent at a low temperature and when unlit might appear to be a thin carbon bracelet. Eleanor came in one morning to see Gigi holding the lamp without its protective chimney, and blowing the delicate precious mantle, soot to her, out the open window.

Unlike the Nehrus of India and others who enjoy separate cuisines of their own and another culture, Granny and Eleanor keep American style kitchens, to which they add Haitian provision and dishes. A family's taste which delights as much in a chowder as a gumbo, knockwurst as fried chicken, rice and grits as potatoes, sweet potato pudding as ice cream, was more appreciative than provincial anyway. It is simple to borrow from the Haitian cuisine marvelous herb sauces, mush and beans, breakfast eggs scrambled with sweet peppers, and the Haitian versatility with rice. With kidney beans it becomes riz et pois, with black mushrooms diri ak djondjon, with hot ti malice sauce, and there are militon and plantain and other native foods tempting with equal gustatory promise.

The Haitian girl who has learned in Eleanor's kitchen knows that her culinary accomplishments will be sought in homes of the educated up and down the mountain. With a year as a fair apprenticeship for the girl, thereby affording help for Eleanor for the constant stream of guests at the mission, a girl is usually able to set the table and bring to it a dish as simple as a poached egg or as provocative as orange soufflé. A few who serve for three years in this cool white kitchen with its old glass in the south window and plants and old china on the divider, who can curry a stew or mold a lobster mousse, manage yogurt or French cream, flip a crêpe or bake a sponge cake, are indeed ready for the embassy. But after showing one how to cook a few dishes, if she does not show promise, Eleanor gives up serving the recipes she cannot handle. Over the years most have become moderately efficient and only legitimately dishonest.

It was finally suggested to Tris after a few weeks of scorching the rice, spilling the soup, burning the bread and breaking the cups that she learn to mop the tiles instead. Not Tris; that was Mona's work. She would just depart. Departed with her the carving knife, the egg beater, and the best enamel pot, but these were only the legitimate perquisites of unfulfilled cooks.

In this learn by doing cue, even the brightest initiate, though painstakingly introduced to the hazards and wonders of a pressure cooker, a meat grinder and a coffee-maker, rarely escapes mishaps, some grievous. There was the day Jeta ignored the gauge that warned of mounting stress within the pressure cooker. Suddenly the heavy lid rose as by atomic thrust, pounded the ceiling like a sudden clap of thunder, pitched back onto the stove with such awesome brunt the burner was smashed. The three horrified keepers of the kitchen, so galvanized to reaction, got the offending hot vessel barehanded through the back door to the yard before the first alarmed member of the household arrived. A denunciation straight from heaven could not have instilled a sharper respect thereafter for the power of gas and electricity.

Rezia was sure she had mastered the relatively simple ritual of making hot tea for guests: Be sure the water is boiling. Pour it over the tea leaves. Let them steep briefly. Strain the tea into the teapot that goes to the table. The mission teapots were ceramic, until a loving friend who knew how often tea regaled guests, gave a silver teapot. And, as guests noted this unexpected touch of elegance, there was added joy in using the pot—until one afternoon Rezia went to bring more tea. There was some tea in the silver pot, so she placed the pot on the gas burner to reheat it. Before her startled eyes, the pot melted.

Neither time nor use has smoothed the strangely scratched surface of a treasured Danish silver serving spoon. This piece Fifi scoured with steel wool.

Joanne, immaculate and naturally luscious as a sun ripe mango, was as wild as a game cock. When she pledged herself to the Christian way, Granny persuaded Eleanor to train her at the house. When she brought the guava jelly to the table so overcooked it pulled like taffy, Wallace's point-blank rejection melted her like seaweed. But, five minutes later, she returned to the head of the table, tittering with laughter, and offered him a crockful of Granny's still warm grapefruit preserves. Joanne did indeed go to the embassy three years later. And her uninhibited histrionics about the house and in the role of Mary Magdalene in the Easter play were missed a great deal more than her light pancakes and fluffy puddings.

Rezia had been given a simple menu, to cook boiled rice and boiled eggs, before she might try something more difficult. Granny came in and looked everywhere for the rice. No rice on the stove, in the stove, or in the cupboard. Finally, she removed the top of the tea kettle. The soft steaming whiteness crowded the inside.

Louise had done very well with potato and rice pudding. Came the day when she must make banana pudding and top it with meringue for a fancier dessert. Two guests from Virginia were giving some money for the tearoom. Granny carefully explained that one fourth cup of sugar must be added slowly while still beating the already stiff egg whites. The banana pudding came to the table with a syrupy goo sliding around the rim of the dish. Louise had simplified the modus operandi by mixing the sugar and whites and beating them together. Generally, if the slightest censure is implied or their importance minimized, they return a question for a question: "Jody, did you bake the pudding?" "Madame, would I serve the pudding unbaked?"

Cosette reeked of garlic but her dignity and cleanliness were unassailable. She went from the mission to a Syrian home that has cherished her talents for an even dozen years.

Dodo is a pearl of great price. Not so young, more European than African, she is the jewel of the mission. Scrupulously well groomed, her gold earrings her one mark of affluence and ancienne noblesse, she gives grace to each duty and performs every service with a professional hand. She is loved at the tearoom.

Riva liked to use her English vocabulary and she found her counterpart in ninety three year old Aunt Virginia who liked to use her Creole when she came to Granny's house. The result was intelligible only to themselves. And no less pleasing to Aunt Virginia, Riva could fix toast and chocolate as temptingly as she could for herself.

Haitian Foods

Many are the fruits and vegetables which can vary a menu in Haiti. Breadfruit came to Haiti as food for the slaves. Captain William Bligh brought three hundred forty-seven trees from Tahiti in 1793. Its starchy texture can be baked, roasted, or fried like a potato.

Banana plants were brought from the Canary Islands by the Spaniards early in the 1500's. This fruit often takes the place of bread in the rural person's diet. The bunch, or stem, is cut green. If left on the stalk to ripen, the flavor is watery and less rich. The old stalk is cut to the ground and a new shoot replaces it next year.

Sweetsop, the custard apple, is deliciously tasty and is usually eaten with a spoon.

Soursop, or corrosol, is pressed for a thick syrupy drink or for ice cream.

Millet, corn, papayas and guavas, mangoes, sour oranges, avocados, limes, coconut, and tamarind flourish where there is adequate moisture. All are inexpensive. The guava makes excellent jelly; the tamarind's acid pulp a cooling drink or sweet preserves.

Bread, which is made from imported flour, oatmeal which comes in tins, butter or margarine, cooking oils, cheese, salt, soap and cleaners are all imported and soon tip the scales the other way.

Cassava is a plant closely related to the poinsettia and the rubber plant. Its fresh roots, inedible until pressed to rid them of the hydrocyanic acid they contain, are the source of tapioca and may be used in making bread.

Granny boils the rind of the grapefruit to rid it of its bitterness, presses the strips, cooks them measure for measure with sugar to make a tasty marmalade called konfiti chadek. Everybody who samples it guesses that it is a tropical fruit, but never grapefruit.

Haitian coffee is unexcelled anywhere. The scarlet berries in clusters are ready to be picked, dried a couple days in the sun, beaten to separate the two halves, and stored. When a handful is to be brewed, the cook pounds the toasted coffee beans in a large wooden mortar with pestle until pulverized. (Mortars and pestles constitute an important investment in Eleanor's kitchen. The smallest are to mince herbs, larger ones to purée, blend or mash, up to one that holds a half gallon of toasted peanuts to be pounded into peanut butter. Most are of lignum vitae, the hardest of the Haitian woods, so hard that the mighty axles used in grinding sugarcane were fashioned from it.)

Hand pollinated vanilla pods, steeped in raw alcohol make superb flavoring. Granny may slip an ample size bottle in the bag of a mission guest as a parting gift.

At the time of year for the logwood (used for dyeing) to be in bloom, bees swarm the golden blossoms like a mist, making Haiti's famous logwood honey.

But the sugarcane is the source of most of the island's saccharine and much of its support. The cane grows along the coast al regions. Primitive high wheel carts, drawn by yokes of plodding oxen, creak in and out of the cane fields, piled high with bundles of sugarcane. These are soon loaded into railroad cars drawn by wood burning locomotives, thence to the outskirts of the city to the sugar mill. Grinding continues here by oxen and wheel, the juice conveyed to huge kettles from which the fragrant aroma of the cooking syrup hangs heavily over the area.

Not food, yet found wherever food is served, are the colorful mats and floor covering made from sisal hemp so important to the economy of the island. The plantations lie near the sea along the coast. For miles the blue-green sea of sword leafed sisal plants are ready to yield their fiber. Sweating ebony bodies in rhythmic motion slash the four foot long leaves which are bundled to be carried to the mill where the fiber can be separated from the stems. Then the white fiber is baled to be shipped to New Orleans, New York and other ports, to be made into mattresses, automobile cushions, upholstery, binder twine, and rope. The green waste is made into tow, to become bags and floor covering.

More Foibles

At the mission, Haitian tiles endow every floor with permanence and smoothness. So indestructible are these cement, colored and pressed handmade tiles, so elegant and durable, they grace palace or wharf with unfailing finesse. Other coverings and textures that confuse cleaning and offer concealment for bugs and their ilk are sparse and little missed.

Almost before a housemaid can sort the uses of broom, mop and dust cloth, she learns that any small thing that crawls, flies, clings, or chews is forthwith dispatched. At times ceaseless vigilance fails to avert sudden and troublesome, sometimes embarrassing, invasions, if bomb and spray are not kept busy. One morning Sudi was soaking strings in kerosene. She was sure madame would want them tied across the door sills to discourage the migration of some small things that crawl. A few nights before, her uncle, attending the leadership conference at the mission, had shared his hostel bed with five visiting cousins, as an after crop of vermin attested.

When the girls earn a little money, they want clothes first, then things. If married, they hound their husbands mercilessly for something gold—earrings first, then a ring or necklace. Rose occupied the position of wash maid, indeed one of the most important at the mission. No one had had time to teach Rose, and it was fortunate that she could adapt to tubs after doing clothes with a paddle all her life in the stream below. She would squat by the tubs, humming, burping, and sloshing her arms up and down, till the dirtiest clothes emerged spotless. And when it came to wielding the charcoal iron, she could iron to perfection. Rose came to work one morning wearing gold earrings. She was the dusky hue of taverneau wood, and as smoothly endowed. More than once her deft ways and spicy manner had stirred a hint of envy. The earrings inspired conspiracy in the laundry. The next morning Rose interrupted Granny's learners, class visibly upset. Injecting venom in an otherwise tranquil morning, she explained, "Jetée and Carmen tell Christians I bad woman. I work at Madame Will's house tomorrow."

But to covet is no less a characteristic of the Haitian male. However, if temptation goes by any other name in Haiti, it is gambling first. He gambles, he borrows, and he covets. It is common practice for two or more males to pool their earnings and take turns at the whole lot. It is hard to blame them when all their lives their wants have never run to more than actual needs; possessions are rarely greater than tools for livelihood.

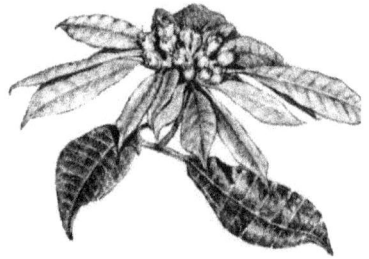

Yet where there is work and the day is sunny, sounds betray lightheartedness and joie de vivre throughout the mission compound: Antoine washing the station wagon with a happy bonjou for every comer and goer; Fortune humming and clipping the grass; Dieula and Rose on the kitchen steps tittering and scraping potatoes; chatter rising from the hospital cooking area below Zenas' singers practicing How Do I Love Thee at the church; Granny welcoming a handful of Michigan tourists.

At Granny's House

Zenas recalls a time when Granny's house sheltered nineteen guests from churches back in Michigan. There was a cot or a bed for everyone but Granny and Zenas, who had come up from Limbé to help with the retreat.

Two beds could be managed in Granny's basement, so there was nothing else but Granny and Zenas should spend the night down there. Granny's basement is the garden level of a house which in American suburbia would be split-level. The top level drops directly off the driveway, which melts in cool shadiness toward the Turnbull house, all but hidden by poinsettias, hibiscus, and guava trees. The garden level stays for a little terrace, then glides sharply all the way to the lily pond. That night, Zenas recalled, a wide arch of stars glittered overhead, a full moon hung low over the western horizon, and eucalyptus, geranium, calla lilies and roses cascading over the stone wall drenched the tropical night with sensuous and exotic fragrance. Now and then a dog barking, the quaver of a Renault on the distant mountain road, the incidental note of a cricket, these and the settling voices in the rooms above were the only night noises.

Granny worked the length of a sheet through the water pipes overhead, and, as she let it fall to make a curtain between the two narrow beds, Zenas raised his right hand to meet hers. Chuckling with mock solemnity, both vowed to respect the curtain, then settled to sleep.

These mission retreats brought much needed awareness and support as Haiti entered more and more into the prayers of churches and individuals, and the work continued to grow.

Once, Granny remembered, there were thirty six guests. Wallace and Eleanor were on one of their back country trips, and Granny had the three little boys. She didn't have a dining room then, and only curtains for doors. But she cooked for the whole crowd and kept dispensary days. "We had a good time, and God blessed us."

She was "Granny" to other missionary families, like the Forrest Sherwoods isolated on the south coast. Each year Mr. Sherwood would have to leave his family behind as he traveled the long, difficult, horseshoe shaped route past Port-au-Prince to an outstation near the Dominican border, where he spent a week at the harvest festival, performed marriage rites, baptized and ministered to the spiritual needs. "That week in every year," he wrote, "it seemed that the devil struck in our family in some way, until I began taking the children up to Fermathe. We were blessed to have a wonderful, loving Granny there in Haiti. Then, after we were back in Iowa, Granny was in our home. After a strenuous day and much visiting, she needed sleep. The next morning we asked how she had slept. 'Oh, fine. I just tell the Lord I need rest, and He giveth his beloved sleep (Psalm 127:2)'."

Again in 1961 it was Granny's turn to keep things going while Eleanor and Wallace were in the States. Some friends recall arriving at the mission early in the morning, and finding Granny baking a wedding cake. Soon the couple arrived with their certificate, and the Reverend Oren Bell, Pignon missionary also visiting the compound, conducted the ceremony. All helped make the day special by giving small gifts to the couple. Granny gave the bride and groom shoes, a blanket, and some one gallon size tin cans for cook pots. The cans would be their most prized gift of all.

Water Again

Needed and fulfilled, now on a mountainous tropical isle, Granny's life pattern grew sterner for one dominant reason: water governs the quality of life and work for all at the mission. Despite all its coast line exposure to water, it is sea water, and Haiti is a thirsty land. When Granny's best handmade cloth or Eleanor's embroidered linens appear on the dinner table, not every guest pauses to appreciate the compliment implied, but most can avow that in the water that launders these nice things abides the noblesse oblige. Together with the soil, water here is the very foundation of existence, and must be conserved, every drop that falls, even when it rains every day during the rainy season. This enormously important lode of wisdom had challenged every aspect of Wally's engineering talent and training from the day he arrived in Haiti. Without one piece of sophisticated equipment, but grateful for the lowly pick and shovel and willing native brawn, he devised and tested a method of water storage that even the rural families could afford.

The first quadrangular cistern was dug out of the limestone next to the first three rooms. The walls had to be thick enough to withstand the pressure of several thousand gallons of water, nine hundred pounds per square foot, and sealed solid against seepage. The walls were as thick as a catacomb and the capacity less than Wally had calculated, but the reservoir held, and does hold to this day, connected to a second, and it to a third, to a fourth, to a fifth, to a sixth, and to a seventh, as rock has been hewn out and laid.

When the first reservoir becomes empty, Wallace goes and manually connects the next to the pump. Gravity takes care of all the flow of water to the laundry, the hospital kitchen, and the hostelry, all of which are on the level below the living area. Only water from the roof is carried into the reservoirs; all surface water is excluded. Granny's house, the guest houses, the hospital, the church, all roofed structures in the compound, are similarly provided with reservoirs, their walls plastered with cement and sealed. Only a mole with his own canteen could find his way around this labyrinth of cuboidal cisterns.

Invariably, the December to March dry season coincides with the Stateside freshet of winter visitors. Always Granny's house, like a Haitian camion with room for one more, has been a haven for ill and weary missionaries from the hot coastal areas, for retreats for the outlying church leaders, for student helpers, and for all denominational groups. Come the board from Grand Rapids, Michigan, an amiable Methodist group building a Methodist mission, a caravan of Moravians, and the Translinear developers from Tortuga. Sometimes the stream is constant. Wives of engineers and contractors are glad for social contacts and the wholesome story hour for their children. Now and again the captain of a U.S. ship will bring a navy Handclasp shipment of school and medical supplies and tarry to visit and lunch. "It's tea and toilet for all of them," Eleanor smiles, pouring anise, spearmint, jasmine, orange pekoe, or citronelle from as many gay colored teapots. And it is an American Standard flush whether at the tearoom or at Granny's house.

A house guest learns to economize with water at any cost. When the water goes off, be it only for a few minutes, the message is clear. Wallace is changing over the valves from the last empty reservoir to the next filled one. Have they ever run out of water? Oh, many times... Better to sponge this morning, and again tonight, even if you have eaten the white dust of an overloaded camion you could not pass from St. Marc to Duvalierville, and your polished healthy tan and new hairdo are gray corduroy and thatch after touring the island all day, rather than use three precious gallons under the shower. The extravagance of flushing haunts the American guest, plenty oriented, for weeks afterward. When one hears Wallace admonish David and Chris, "And don't shave with running water," one does not let it run to brush teeth or coax hot water. One welcomes with éclat the temperature the spigot delivers, and cuts his stay in the bathroom so his neighbor across the way makes it on time to the breakfast table too.

Sister Joan Margaret

When Granny reached fourscore years, an aura began to glow around her birth date. Not that it slowed her especially; friends just began noticing how little her auburn hair had silvered and how much she continued to do each day. No acknowledgment of the day makes her happier than when Sister Joan Margaret brings her blind girls up to the mission to sing for her.

Sister Joan Margaret, a bantam sized little dynamo, runs an Episcopalian school in Port-au-Prince for handicapped children, a couple of hundred or more, many of them blind from malnutrition in infancy. About twenty of these children have learned to play instruments which they put together into an orchestra. So, on May 7, two publiques of clarinets, trumpets, violins, bass violins, drums, and children arrive at Fermathe about midmorning. They set up on the playground because everybody on the place whose job will spare him, gathers for this remarkable concert. Granny sits and wipes a tear as she listens to their repertoire of classical selections, Haitian folk songs, and Granny's favorite hymns. He Leadeth Me touches her most, its words her own prayer of daily dedication.

Lord, I would clasp my hand in Thine
Nor ever murmur or repine
Content whatever lot I see
Since 'tis God's hand that leadeth me...

Where but in Haiti

Early impressions done by Eleanor

Riva and Timene

The night is black. The long necked rêle bird repeats its eerie cry in the ravine below. The dark mysterious mountains tower around.

A sixteen year old girl has died. For the all-night vey men sit in small groups about the yard, not engaging in low talk, but dealing the cards or throwing dice, their voices unrestrained. Fumes of clairin, the fulsome local grog, rest on the warm air.

Under a freshly erected palm leaf arbor, the young dance to the rhythm of the drums. Occasionally one breaks apart in a frenzied whorl, throws his head far back and emits a shriek of such horrendous stridor it rends the night in one long wail that lasts until his head has made a gyre to his toes. Off to one side, rice and beans bought with borrowed money cook in a big black pot. Local custom prescribes that mourners be fed.

Outside the door of the little thatch-roofed hut, the neighbor women sell biscuits and candies from large wooden trays. Inside, all is quiet. The light from a tin lamp flickers over the corpse of the young girl, sitting upright on a chair in a corner. A virgin, she is dressed in white with a halo of flowers on her head, her board-like legs supported by new white shoes too heavy for her lifeless feet. The father sits in the opposite corner, sunken-eyed, staring at the damp earth floor. The mother, close to the corpse, smooths the white dress and occasionally groans in agonizing grief.

The hours wear on. A chill breeze rising with the dawn blows in with the chanting, wailing, and cursing of the mourners. An old woman gently pushes open the plank door, then closes it behind herself against the morning light and sounds outside. She drops down beside the dead girl's mother. A small book in her hand, she speaks softly, "Riva, do you remember what Jesus said, 'He that believeth in me, though he were dead, yet shall he live'?" The woman, as if returning from another world, murmurs, "Yes, Granny, in your classes... and Pastor Simon has told us many times..."

Riva, unlike her neighbor Timene, felt herself too poor to afford the white man's god.

Being a merchant, or more aptly, a restauranteur, Timene and her seven children show signs of enjoying more and better food than their neighbors. Even now several customers wait for her to drop fresh batter in the sizzling, garlic spiced oil, then watch the fritters puff up, writhe, twist and turn golden brown. Folks like the red pepper vinegar and oil sauce Timene serves with her cod fritters.

The old iron bell of nearby St. Jacques sounds the call to morning mass. Bong, clang, it echoes across the ravines.

Timene straightens from her squatting position, takes the iron pot of hot oil from the three stones, smiles as she hands the fritters on banana leaves. Her black face is unblemished except for a round scar the size of a Haitian two cent piece, low on the left cheek— avouchment of the hot coin used by the bocor at her initiation into the local Voodoo society. It explains the fear and apprehension in her eyes, and the cross nail ouanga tied with red and black cord around her neck. It explains the scent of cinnamon-spiced rum on the air. She has just poured out the rum in four directions to her gods.

Now she rubs her hands and feet with the sacred spiced rum. And fumbling the cross nail ouanga, she tucks it deep inside her coarse denim dress, as though asking leave of her loa, and goes to answer the call of the bell at St. Jacques' chapel.

The Pageant

It was Sunday. Soimeus, looking elegant even in his faded green shirt, his face full of rapture, greeted the gathering congregation. "Madame taught me to read the Word," he smiled beatifically.

Soon he was preaching. "Ah, but you're just morning glory Christians when you let Satan tempt you. You close up when the sun is hot. You learned to walk in the mud and not fall for caution. Now you walk where it's dry but fall from carelessness.

"You wash your hands, then wipe them on the ground. You're like the woman victim who stood in line to get oil. We saw her bottle was dirty and refused to put in the oil. Oh, Lord, we come asking You to cleanse us before You put in Your oil."

The crooning chorus of amens was manifestly impatient. Late comers had continued to filter in until an eager body was wedged into every inch of space. Windows and doors were filled. The congregation was now settled, two-deep, for the Christmas program. Loulon had trained the boys to sing, and the occasion was enough to let themselves go. Soon their lusty singing bespoke the liberation of their undernourished souls. Their voices rang around the mountainside.

The adult choir, half hidden behind the stage, became the angel host. Shepherds eased through the banana fronds in search of the Christ Child. Came the three kings from the East. Then came a pilgrim seeking the Child. He called his wife to bring his macoute (bag) and his fighting cock to take as his gifts.

Soon the pilgrim was stopped by a beggar. No, said he, all he had would be gifts for the Christ Child. But the stranger begged for his own sick child. Pray, wouldn't the pilgrim save his child? Whereupon he was given the rooster.

Hardly had he started on his way again when a woman with a baby stopped this man and pled for food for her starving infant. He moved ahead but she walked backwards, pleading insistently, hitching her skirt tighter and projecting her hunger pangs with such emotional authenticity, many in the congregation were in tears. All were deeply moved. They had all lived through years of drought and want. Despite the restored condition of all now with enough to eat, such display of distress evoked empathy that was real. No cold and dispirited audience was this. The pilgrim gave the woman his macoute and started on his way again. He was soon accosted by an old man needing shoes. Trying to move on, the pilgrim felt the old man's clutch and torment and looked upon his extended bruised and bleeding feet. To sighs of approval, he took off and gave the old man his own shoes. The reader said, Inasmuch as ye have done it unto these, ye have done it unto me.

The pilgrim faded into the crowd. Mary made her way up the aisle on a little burro, followed by Joseph. Together they knelt at the Christ Child's manger. All the flock joined in this dramatic climax singing with heartfelt fervor, Silent Night, Holy Night, while Soimeus urged the unsaved to come to the Lord. Many did.

The three wise men appear in mission Christmas decorations with calabash (gourd) heads and basket bodies.

This program had been given two or three times before this Sunday. First, it was given before a conclave of all the missionaries on the island, then at the church on Christmas Eve. If a player dropped out, a stand-in could assume the role with such perfect negroid theatricals that never a muff marred the performance. More likely, a new twist would appear with eloquent pith, and, like Granny's Christmas cards, the play lost none of its attraction no matter when or how often it was performed.

There had to be something after the pageant for each child, if only a piece of candy. Granny had managed.

There had to be milk and eggs and patience if the little taboo ridden, potbellied waif, abandoned at the hospital yesterday, returns to health. Granny is managing.

There had to be enough food for new converts C'est Tout and Nazilus when they come to work in the morning, their stomachs empty. Granny will manage.

And, unless Granny's prayers go unanswered, there must be others ready to hazard a Lord send me to ease this land's pain.

"Jesus said to tarry and work until He comes," Granny quoted with literal acceptance. "It may be soon," she added with more than a hint of expectancy.

The Cockfight

Nothing in all Haiti nurtures the village men's weakness for gambling like the weekly cockfight contest. Each area has its pros and its permanent ring. Constructed squarely, or nearly so, of poles, roofed like his hut, it is surrounded by a sprawling seat rail of poles on which the wildly gyrating spectators more often stand than sit. The crowd is always dense close to the ring, chiefly those who are ready to hazard their week's earnings on the home cock.

Rivalry never runs so high as when a Kenscoff cock is pitted against one of a smaller village like Fermathe. The Fermathe ring, moreover, is hardly a stone's throw up the mountain from the church.

Time for the match brings on a fever of betting. Visiting spectators crowd the opposing side of the ring. Exchanges of insults, ridicule, twitting taunts and ribald thrusts mount to a wild frenzy. At length the visiting cock will be led forth and with rambunctious gesticulation his prowess proclaimed. Then a challenge is accepted and the home cock is admitted to the ring with even more holding forth. The two cocks are inspected for match in weight and size, and after some more dickering, the two cocks begin fighting. The owners resort to every contortion and sound to intensify the fray.

Before a match the witch doctor is paid to forecast the victor. Then a round-the-clock surveillance ensures that no one bewitches the cock. On the afternoon prior to the fight, the owners agree to stop the fight when the risk of serious injury and death seems inevitable in the ring. Like a race horse or greyhound, these birds are groomed by skilled caretakers. They are expensive, corn-fed, well trained, and taken to the witch doctor's peristyle to be blessed.

And the cocks are not without their own strategy. To overawe his opponent, the grey will whirl with lightning speed, shake his feathers, limber up and drop his wings. Red darts forward, fiercely pecks his opponent, does a half circle, backs away, lowers his head, raises the feathers on his neck, advances again. Their movements resemble a dance routine. Grey springs forward and the two grapple and lock bills, and hold.

The din of the spectators rages. There is a wild flutter of wings, the struggle continues, attack and counterattack, as if in a death match. The crowd rampages as the visiting Grey presses the home Red to the edge of the ring. Red's owner desperately sprays rum in a reviving mist from his mouth. The expedient is enough, for this time Red recovers and drives Grey to the opposite end of the ring.

When both cocks become so battle weary that their forays begin lagging, their owners spray mouthfuls of rum, hiss, stomp, and contort their bodies, the clamor of the crowd now a wild tumult. The cocks, heads are bloody blobs, their long tail feathers dragging the dust, their movements drunken. Since the life and eyes of the cocks must be spared, the two are spurred to one last effort, which usually puts one on the run and the pursuer is declared the victor. The owners quickly pick up their birds, spray their heads with liquor, then thrust them into their mouths to suck the blood from the battered little heads. This hastens recovery. Bets are settled, and if the night is young, another fight is as fanatically followed.

Only the men attend the cockfights. Although strictly male oriented, the sport dominates more than one aspect of Haitian culture—art in particular. One finds the cock in wood carvings, paintings, and sculptures. His bright color has a place in the decor of an exclusive restaurant, on a camion, or in a hand blocked fabric. He is to Haiti as the bull is to Spain.

Weddings

Tomorrow Renée will be wed, and before each hut sit women preparing their hairdos.

Haitian women contrive original and intricate hairdos. About once a week the young Haitian girl sits on a straw mat in front of her hut, leaning against the knees of a sister or friend who goes through her woolly mop first with her fingers then with a wide toothed comb. Then she oils and fashions it.

In rural Haitian society matrimony poses considerable financial difficulty, hence a kind of common-law marriage substitutes until a couple accumulates enough money to pay for the wedding feast dictated by social tradition. Only in recent years has the influence of missions induced young people to begin their life together with a simple wedding ceremony. Granny always saves face and funds for a young bridegroom convert by baking the wedding cake, and often mission guests chip in with gifts.

Since the burden of expense rests on the bridegroom, it might be several years before he can afford the traditional feast of chicken and rum and dancing, and, often as not three or more of the couple's children are there to join them in their rites. Sometimes a family of eight or ten children will participate when the man or woman, or both, become Christian.

For a wedding of a fairly affluent couple asking a Christian ceremony, one may readily recognize Western influence in the proceedings. Renée's wedding is one of these.

The choir assembles. Most of the pews are filled, a more than convivial titter of expectancy churning the morning air with the palm leaf fans. A dozen or so little girls in white skirts sashay down the aisle. Soon, as many maidens, pretty, flip and impudent in bright blue or shocking pink dresses, pair off with white shirt and bow tie young men at the church door,

After a sister of friend fashions her hair-do the Haitian girl becomes in turn hairdresser. Tomorrow René will be wed.

and self consciously move down the aisle to the front.

The bride and groom enter together and sit in chairs, while two witnesses (more or less godparents) sit or stand behind them. The lady witness is also lady in waiting and keeps the bride's veil and skirt spread out without a wrinkle. If the air is unduly warm, she will fan the bride with her palmetto fan.

The congregation enjoys a season of lusty evangelistic singing.

With the last refrain of *Bringing in the Sheaves*, a little one tumbles from the bench and a dozen or more guests rise from their seats to restore her. A choir member reaches the whimpering little miss first, hands her over a couple of rows and deposits her beside a big sister.

Loulon, in his Sunday best, at length rises with practiced graciousness and begins the very ritual Granny has taught him.

"Brothers and Sisters, we are gathered here today in this holy

place to see our young brother and sister joined in the holy bonds of wedlock..."

Afterward Granny's wedding cake is large enough that everyone gets a piece with some tea.

The newlyweds will have three stones and a pot for cooking, a gourd or two, a straw mat, a little wooden bed, a table, four chairs, and a little cupboard, most prized of all. After all, three rocks, a pot, and a mortar and pestle are enough to set up housekeeping, so this couple is more affluent than most. They will also share a small Creole Bible, for both came up in the mission school and can read.

The failing light tints the landscape pale rose, after a day of fête noces (celebration), then a deep red, as creeping shadows shape and reshape the forms of villagers returning to their huts. A faint afterglow lingers in the west with the gentle Bon soirs of the thinning number along the road.

The holy rites may not every time sanctify youthful romance and promise. A decency needful before baptism, ceremonies for unwed couples with grown children and even grandchildren are common. Only Teko has been able to bring to his wedding celebration thirty six children, their children and grandchildren. Granny sat and murmured the benediction with Toulon as he pronounced the mellowed couple man and wife. Teko's walk with his Maker, though not as close as Enoch's, held out until he was 113. His funeral was on Christmas Eve.

The Markets

*Their head loads are so heavy,
two men may have had to heave
the basket from the ground.*

Any visitor to Haiti is soon aware of women laden with baskets on their heads on every road and trail. If you are awake, you will hear the women long before dawn, as early as three thirty, moving briskly along both sides of the main roads to all of the cities of the island. Their destination is most likely the capitol city whose markets are rivaled only by Duvalierville. These women move in rather silent columns until day begins to break and they can glimpse the city around the next curve. Then they stride with such happy chatter and laughter that they are called Madame Sara, after the flocks of bright yellow and black canaries that warble and chirp so noisily they drown out all other sounds.

Some of these women may walk barefooted two or three days over rough trails in the hot sun, carrying loads of eighty pounds on their heads, and return home with no more than seventy cents. They will make the trip twice a week. Some may push a donkey so heavily laden he is all but hidden by the baskets, then sit astride the little beast on the return trip. Those who carry wooden trays rest them on their heads, a doughnut of twisted cloth (torque) cushioning the load. After years of carrying heavy burdens the skull becomes depressed around the extruded top of the head. Another twisted square of cloth girds their waists to give pull. These women are the produce market of Haiti, and most of them are blessed with slim waists, shapely hips, and erect, graceful carriage.

For the burro, life knows no frolic. When he's not making the trip to market, he may stand while a banana farmer up the mountain cuts the stems with his machete and swings the heavy fruit on his back. Or, down in the city where construction is going on, he may carry sand and cement in a day long shuttle.

Nothing is quite so overwhelming as the business of vending in Port-au-Prince. The famous Iron Market there is under one vast expanse of roof supported by iron columns, the façade unlike any other architecture on the island. During French rule, iron grilles were ordered cast by a Pittsburgh foundry. About the same time an Indian rajah commissioned iron columns from the same foundry. When shipped, the two orders were exchanged. The grilles went to India, the columns to Haiti. Adaptation rather than another turn with time and fortune settled the error. Permanent stalls overflow with mountains of straw hats, stacks of sisal mats, thousands of carved Haitian figures, countless leather sandals, rush-seated chairs, paintings, boxes and bins of buttons, strings of Job's tears beads dyed red, blue, green, old glass, books, gaudy lithographs, magazines, all a monstrous shamble through which the tourist shops. You buy some baskets or mats which will indelibly tag you as a tourist, to be followed by relentless vendors. "Madame, fifty cents," for a small lacquer box; five dollars for a small painting, forty for one larger (that will go for ten with a little bargaining).

The aisles are so narrow, vendor and shopper boggle in the stiflingly overcrowded half-light. Sense of smell is assaulted by sweat, urine, and produce. Above all is the familiar din, the unmistakable quality of Africa.

Outside in the shimmering heat, you step into a sea of multicolored chemises and scarves, cheap housewares, pieces of chintz and vinyl, mats and baskets, trays of baked goods, all of which overflows into the street, eventually stalling traffic in one huge chaotic jam. Now a determined truck driver, his bed piled high with black heads like a mound of black grapes, starts moving anyway, and honks the way open again.

On the Waterfront

More incredible is the open-air market on the waterfront, amid a seething ant heap of people, where everything is on the ground, shaded by palm thatched shelters. The din, the congestion, the pungent smells, the offering of everything edible, wearable and usable within the penny economy and imagination of the Haitian to barter or sell, you have found it. Yams by the pile, cinnamon bark, colored yarn, nails, soap, bluing, native millet, rice and meal in neat mounds on squares of paper, a twist of spices, or a bit of pork frying over a charcoal brazier, a dubious colored drink, a strap for your sandal, the choice is yours for a few cents.

Another Open Air Market

The market at Pont l'Estere is also open-air, and brings literally thousands of villagers from all over the Artibonite Valley. Let your station wagon cool off while you consider some eggplant, and vendors will swarm around, thrusting their heads inside the car with their wares. You get out to inspect the mounds of manioc, small squash, okra, tomatoes, garlic, bananas, papayas, mangoes, oranges, limes, grapefruit, shadoc (cross of orange and grapefruit) spread on mats on the ground. Squatting on low stools or resting Hindu fashion on their haunches, snugly turbaned women guide you to their wares. Clothes baskets filled with calabashes all but hide little donkeys patient under their load. These gourds fill every demand for pot and pan and pail. The story holds that after the expulsion of the French in 1803, Henri Christophe requisitioned all the calabashes in the land, and when the small farmers brought their coffee to the markets, they were paid in these coveted gourds. Hence, the Haitian coin corresponding to a franc is called a gourde.

The educated with sleek hairdo, gold earrings and necklace, haggles along with the nun and occasional blan (white tourist). The buyer's status actually depends on the wit and humor he brings to the haggle. The Haitians love a blan like Eleanor who speaks their language and can trade insults with them. If the tourist accedes too readily, the vendor might do his haggling for him and present him with what he considers a fair bargain. A woman chooses three luscious mangoes and makes a price. Then she, amid more banter, insists that another little one be added for the bonus (degi). The vendor protests, more exchanges follow, until there is split the difference, with the woman taking the three mangoes and a small avocado.

You may tangle with a pig's or goat's tether, bump the turkeys, and chickens' baskets; you may move away from a girl in a trance, her sponsor seeking the witch doctor's fee from any who will give a cent. On your way home, you will skirt rice drying along the roadside in the sun and see women washing themselves, their clothes and their children in every stream.

It is no uncommon sight in Haiti to see women winnowing millet by the roadside.

The Voodoo Drums

"We teach them better farming so they will have food; we teach them sanitation so they will be less disease ridden; we teach them to read and write so the supernatural will lose its hold of them; but if we don't teach them to accept a 'Lord, I believe' spiritual change, they will continue to be slaves to superstition and a prey to the unscrupulous. Fear is the essence of primitive religion," insisted Wallace.

T here were Guests as usual that evening.
"Beyond all this is something else," Uncle Zenas was saying. "Fatalism! Their children die, storms erode their lands, destroy their crops. 'The good God so willed it' (aloud), then they allude to the appeased spirits and neglected ceremonies in a whisper."

"Voodoo. How real this is to them, how ingrained into their being, nobody can really understand," added Wallace. "I began trying to understand more than thirty years ago when every night there floated up to us the mingling sounds of tom-toms, the skirl of flutes and conch shell trumpets, the insistent drumming of the Voodoo dance and the plaintive thread of native chants; when we saw goat skulls, powders, potions, beads and charms sold openly in the marketplace: and knew they observed Voodoo fêtes throughout the year."

"And those times when they travel miles to a sacred grotto or a cliff in the mountains, their festivals veiled in mystery," added Granny, "and the gayest of all, noisiest and most colorful, Mardi Gras. The Haitian version of this otherwise Catholic carnival weaves folklore and Voodoo and rum into dance and song wildly unlike anything you'll see in this hemisphere. This endlessly repetitious show of parade and costume, dance and song, beat of drums and blare of trumpets goes on many weekends. Then it ends up in front of the Presidential Palace in one big blast on the last day. This is mainly an excess of the common people; the educated celebrate in their private homes with balls and house parties, aloof from the street dancing."

"A mixture of Christianity and Voodoo, their revelry actually carries through half the year," Eleanor added. "After the festivities in January they begin preparing for Mardi Gras, which culminates in Rara for three days, Good Friday through Easter Sunday when Judas is put to death. Then, there's nothing like the pilgrimage in July to the grotto and waterfall of Saut'd Eau for a totally pagan ritual under the falls and the sacred giant mapou tree.

"At Easter and at Christmas we are hard pressed here at the mission to present these traditionally most Christian observances. We do it in pantomime to hold the Christian youth while all the street madness is going on. We climax a four day Bible school with a pageant in which they work off their fervor. They perform with such native histrionics that a packed sanctuary joins in their melodrama with delirious hallelujahs. This way we wonder far less than the Catholic priest, who claims several thousand Easter communicants, how many are secret followers of Voodoo."

"The Haitians are great on drama and display," Wally, carried the point. "Their songs in Creole as well as plays. We see that each one has a part and gets to march on and off the stage. This delights them. Very few fail to have a flair for acting and they put themselves in their roles without self-consciousness. And they build up excited participation over any common effort that stirs their imagination and emotion."

"Tell us about the time you went to a Voodoo ceremony and we'll let you off doing penance," said Chris to Zenas.

Zenas Relates Voodoo Ceremony

One evening I said to Gilbert, my friend who has the Seashell, that I'd like to go sometime. He told me to see a priestess whom I'd find deep in the heart of the city. Her powers had passed to her from her father, a witch doctor whom even I'd heard about. When I appeared at her peristyle, Madame Frederique returned my Bon soir with a Sphinx-like calm, never taking her eyes off me. In the dimness behind her I could see machetes and pipes and charms and rows of ancient looking bottles and earthen jars crowding the walls of her living quarters. No doubt the strange malodor hanging over the place emanated from those potions in the jars.

When I mentioned Gilbert's name she warmed a little and after we'd talked awhile she told me of a ceremony that same evening only a few miles above here at Kenscoff. Then she told me what to say to the priest when I got there.

Long before I reached the tonelle—this is a thatched shelter on poles less elaborate than a peristyle—I heard the familiar beat of the Rada drums. For the Voodoo worshiper the drum is more than a sacred instrument; it is the vessel of deity. (Remember the day Victor stole his family's drums and they all fell to the ground wailing that their gods couldn't speak to them, that they couldn't hear their gods voices!) There are always three drums. Each is made with taut skins anchored by wooden pegs or rope over heavy oak frames. The largest is played with a hammer-shaped stick which yields a terrific vibration. The middle drum is played with two sticks a straight one and a bowed one. The smallest drum gives a shallow note from two sticks used for a fast beat. Drumming precedes a ceremony for a long time then intensifies as the crowd gathers and dancing commences. The varied beats bear the names of long ago African originators and these beats govern the steps and movements of the dancers.

In the semidarkness there were probably fifty people standing or sitting on poles. I murmured Bon soir and edged through the gathering to find the priest. When I mentioned Gilbert and Madame Frederique he acknowledged my presence and waved me to a place. He was busy setting up for the ritual. He was doing something with several pottery jars spirit inhabited and some gourd rattles and other of the same fetishes I had seen at Madame Frederique's and to one side of the tonelle an attendant was cooking something in a pot over a bed of glowing coals. Twice a live chicken was sacrificed and added to the mixture the entrails put aside. Meanwhile the ritual had warmed up. There were three would-be initiates or candidates whom the priest would bring out of his hut for awhile one then all three, and put them through an awesome performance. With startling agility they would dance with candles, then machetes, then ropes of beads all the time chanting. Their dance gradually became more excited and more complex. The night was cool but their bodies glistened with sweat. As the routine increased they chanted in circles leaping and whirling and growing louder with their chant. It became a surge of sound that droned with a vague foreboding mournful mystery.

Then the part I wanted most to see was the symbol drawing. It's done with cornmeal and with an incredible artistry. The drumming subsides for this exhibition. I knew that a serpent predominates but there before our eyes on the ground those three initiates fashioned in cornmeal a marvelously intricate serpent, then a ship, a cross, a machete, a flag, and finally the sign of the crossroads. I was transfixed by it all, it was done so expertly. These are the banners of their gods, or loas. The serpent god and the sea god (ship) seem to be the most important. They are the same loas worshipped by the Ibo tribe of West Africa, their forebears, and they are the same rites practiced by the slaves who worked the French plantations. However, there are traces of influence by the Indians who inhabited this island and were absorbed by the Spanish and French. And Christianity's unmistakable symbol of the cross was not omitted. All these symbols were inspected and approved by the Houngan who blessed them with rum and the sacrifice of a chicken.

There was more frenzied dancing thunderous drumming, and the ritual drawing, called vever, was obliterated by the dancers feet. Then there were intoned prayers and some portions of the Catholic mass.

I'd heard about the rituals with fire. Too often a badly burned participant had been brought to the hospital. But before the contents of the pot were apportioned out for refreshment for a gourde, on papaya and banana leaves, a bevy of young girls varied the dance routine. The girls danced with an easy, laughing grace. They were all in starched skirts, and their leader clung to one of the three who had passed the initiation. Together they passed under a fiery hot rod no more than eighteen inches from the ground. Then one of the girls became possessed. Seizures or possession can be accomplished by a rapid breathing in or gasping that increases the oxygen intake and diminishes the carbon dioxide in the lungs. This produces dizziness and hyperventilation or an auto-hypnotic state that permits the one possessed to writhe in a fixed sort of rhythm. The sister dancers quickly picked her up and carried her into the inner sanctum, or hounfor. This possession is common. You may see it in the marketplace. Someone has to pay the witch doctor to release her from her trance. We can only speculate that some sort of drug keeps her that way a day or so.

The climactic ritual took place over the live coals when the pot was emptied. The three initiates, still veiled, actually trod upon those live coals and then passed them through their hands. Their feet were bare, of course, and there was not the least twinge or cry of pain. These girls have a thick callous on the soles of their feet, but had they had a painkiller or some sort of insulation? I had to remind myself that I've seen Dieula dip her bare hand in a pot of boiling water to bring forth boiled eggs. The men in their ritual then stooped and struck their bare feet hard on the ground. They stamped and sawed the air and leaped high, sweat running in rivulets down their bodies. Impervious to fatigue they chanted and danced as if driven by some inexorable compulsion. Well, all of this went on repetitiously until the gray dawn. I stayed through it all—a purgatorial din.

"Once was enough for me," sighed Zenas. "There is a deep and profound meaning through it all. As the night and ritual dwindled into a thick sob with the drums, my compassion sobbed with it. No other sight or sound in this primitive land had so stirred me. And no less acute is the pain whenever I lie in bed and hear those Rada drums. I was exhausted awaiting the agony of the last subsiding pulse, and because I grew up hearing those drums, I thought I was insulated."

The waupon tree, sacred to Voodoo worshipers, is wound in vari-colored cords by suppliants during festival rites.

Breaking the thoughtful silence that followed, Chris described his pilgrimage to the waterfall:

If there is meaning, there must also be construction. The chief god Damballah Wedo (snake god) and his mistress Aida Wedo (rainbow) have chosen one of Haiti's most beautiful waterfalls as their home. Last summer David and I traveled by jeep over the mountains of north Haiti and across the muddy central plateau to reach Ville Bonheur, in the heart of the island for the largest of all the Voodoo ceremonies held each year on July 16. Thousands of pilgrims from every part of the republic praying and singing, crowd to the foot of the falls. They stand or splash and dance under the healing violence of the falling water, awestruck in the presence of their gods. When Damballah "mounts" one of them the worshipper trembles and staggers like a drunken man. Fellow worshipers rush to help him out of the water, shake hands and listen to his garbled utterances as an oracle from Damballah. For days they come, the poor on foot, the better off by overloaded camion, the well-to-do in sleek cars some in groups led by a local houngan who can help them communicate their desires and gratitude to Damballah. There in the falls, once a year, one and all seek release from their old contracts with the gods and establish new ones. Multicolored cords wound about the waist symbolize these contracts. When the suppliant emerges, his repeal complete, he winds the cords around a sacred tree. So sacred is the tree that exemption is carried home in a scant thimbleful of the earth around it, to give to those too old or too ill to make the pilgrimage. The pilgrim also drinks his fill of the water and carries as much of it home as he can.

But, lo, Damballah's eminence is not supreme over the waterfall. Bathers who reached the falls at dawn will gather by nine o'clock around the Catholic church. After mass, they haul down Our Lady of Mount Carmel from her niche on the church balcony lower her to the top of a waiting camion and amid a tumult parade her around the village square. The multitude breaks into frenzied wailing, thanksgiving and supplication hubbub and clamor filling the air in one hell's delight. With uplifted palms and burning tapers, for some it is an annual must; for others a once in a lifetime fulfillment.

"Only the Haitian could accept such a juxtaposition of opposing beliefs as Voodoo and Christianity—Catholic Christianity," interposed Wallace.

"How does he do it?" asked Chris.

"Roman Catholicism," began Wallace, "is the religion of state, but it has never been popular because back there a century or more ago the Catholic clergy were injured by their opposition to Freemasonry, for one thing. The Haitian loves the pomp of the order. Another reason may be that there were too many adventurers among the clergy. Those who donned the clerical garb to obtain a lucrative and easy living may also have been expelled from European parishes. The Catholic priest, for a fee, has also been known to bless a temple dedicated to Voodoo worship or charms used in their fetish rites. Such blandness renders him ineffective in contending with Voodoo worship. Too, the Voodoo priest borrows no less from the Catholic Priest. Much of his equipage is identifiable with Christianity. This dates back to the ban by French colonials of Voodoo practice, which simply merged in outward practices with Catholicism. It grows in complexity when political expediency mixes in. 'Papa Doc' Duvalier claimed to be a Catholic, a Protestant, and also a witch doctor.

"So the Voodoo priest burns candles and covers his walls with the saints and the Virgin Mary, while encouraging lascivious dancing, drinking, and indiscriminate sex. But Voodoo is the common man's heritage of a thousand years; it is also his faith in the future. He communes with his gods when he drums and dances and chants, and also with the dead. It is so deeply rooted, it is almost an inextricable part of life for him," Wallace concluded.

"Until he is genuinely brought face to face with the Lord Jesus," offered Uncle Zenas quietly.

Dieula came in with servings of ice cream.

"Corrossol," explained Eleanor. "The fruit is like a lovely green heart with prickly bumps all over it. We mash the pulp for this superb dessert. The juice or milk is a beverage." "And the leaves are mildly sedative," Wallace added. "They're pleasantly soothing in a sick baby's bath."

"Or your own bath when you've been in the jeep all day," confirmed David, who had slipped into his place unnoticed. "Dr. Jim and his wife were in their jeep behind me. They're coming over probably this evening."

"Oh, he's the young doctor over at Albert Schweitzer Hospital who is making a study of medicinal herbs while he's in Haiti," replied Eleanor. "He plans to go into medical research. If they are over at the guest house, I should go over for them."

"They may be with Granny. Antoine came to get Granny a few minutes ago."

The Witch Doctor

"They can do some mighty neat tricks, these witch doctors," began Chris. "Yesterday I saw René place an active, live chicken on the table, then hold his head in his hand a moment, and the chicken fell over dead. A minute or two later, nobody saying anything, he held his hand over his head and the chicken revived. I saw him do it. Then he tucked the chicken under his arm and left, sure that he'd scared the daylights out of somebody there for whom he had a message. How did he do it?"

"Probably with a depressant of some kind, then a stimulant," said Wallace.

"Such as..." began David, and those at the table turned to welcome the Jamiesons whom Granny had brought over from her house. They declined dessert but smiled as Eleanor began pouring tiny cups of Haitian coffee. "He has the answers," pursued David. "He knew what had been given the man down at Petit Goâve who *Greta Cole* couldn't speak but could use his hands."

"You must be talking about our redoubtable confrére, the witch doctor," their last guest joined in the conversation.

"Yes," said Wally, "what plant grows around here that might paralyze the vocal cords?"

"Perhaps Indian poke or mother-in-law tongue," suggested Dr. Jamieson.

"How does he do these tricks?" persisted Chris.

"It would be unfair to classify his practices as tricks," began the doctor, whose willingness to explore the subject suited his hearers:

Despite chicanery and deception, the medicine man from antiquity had complete faith in those practices handed down to him and he has taken pride in his skills. The primitive practice of magic, like our psychotherapy, is based on the power of suggestion—"Nature cures the disease while the remedy amuses the patient"—which accounts for most of the witch doctor's successes. In a sense he comes of a time-honored lineage. His predecessors in the so-called black arts were the priests in the tribe. In their most scrupulous role they were the surgeons and keepers of the healing arts secrets. All narcotics from antiquity have been linked with religion or magic. Species of noxious plants may have been found growing around ancient Inca temple operating rooms—thought to have been used by the priests as anesthetics and pain killers.

"Even after he becomes a Christian, we find the witch doctor reluctant to impart his secrets," confided Wallace.

The guild crosses several lines. The Indian medicine man no doubt exchanged his plants and secrets with the African slave practitioner. Many of the slaves were from advanced African tribes, enemies or captives of a tribal chieftain who grabbed the opportunity to eliminate his rivals by selling them to the slave trader. The calabar bean which yields a potent stimulant comes from Africa, as does the arrow plant, so called because the African hunter could tip his spear with the poison obtained from the seeds, and bring down elephants on the Ivory Coast. Modern medicine has long accepted the drug that is extracted from the herb, called strophantus in treating heart disease. A specific for syphilis has been developed from it. And cortisone is also a derivative.

As one studies the evolution of medicine, similarity of beliefs and practices of medicine men of all cultures around the world convinces one that the primitives of the world shared a common tradition and carried their customs and practices wherever they migrated. The priest or medicine man passed his powers in a hereditary line.

Again, magic art as a method of healing is as old as man himself. The word "magic," coined in Persia, came from the word meaning great or excellent, mah, and was applied to the priest. Since all disease was considered demonic in origin, treatment was directed to casting out the demon by purification with water supplemented by herbal and other therapeutic means. To curtail the powers of demons the poisonous herbs, in particular, were believed to have healing powers. Even after civilization was advanced—in Babylonia, Persia Egypt—the physician who had learned to use natural means of dealing with pathological conditions, still had to compound his treatment with placebos—magic and divination—to please his patient. From antiquity we have inherited demons. Sorcerers claim to command the powers of evil or the evil eye. Astrology interprets the stars as governing the destiny of peoples and individuals.

More or less the same beliefs associated medicine and magic and pervaded all primitive religion except Judaism. The strict monotheistic and hygienic doctrines of Moses prevented the superstitions of the Jews from even approximating those of their neighbors. Even in New Testament times people believed God sent messages through the victim of a seizure, and someone was always on hand to put down what he said, no matter how incoherent, when he was coming out of a convulsion. In Luke, the boy really had epilepsy. If he had been demonstrating in an hysterical convulsion he would not have hurt himself. But it's significant to note that the practice of healing among Hebrews was not in the hands of the priests as it was among Egyptians, Babylonians and Persians. The people of Judea had professional physicians who separated priesthood from magic 450 years before Hippocrates. The distinction in the Old Testament lay in social hygiene. The keystone of Mosaic Law was the interdependence of physical and mental purity. Moses precepts were sound. Strict sanitary and dietary regulations spared the Hebrew from many of the diseases suffered by his neighbors. Of course Moses was trained in all the wisdom of the Egyptians which included medicine. And from their papyri the Egyptians bound all their religion with magic. Yet they excelled in hygiene. The priests set the example of strict cleanliness. Because hair attracts dirt, they shaved their heads and entire bodies every third day. They lived an almost aquatic existence. They bathed twice daily and twice nightly.

"But the ancient Hebrews also had herbs," insisted Chris. "Frankincense and myrrh were actually medicinal, weren't they?"

Yes. The lure to find plants goes beyond 1,500 years B.C., about the time of Moses, when Queen Hatspur of Egypt sent ships to the Land of Punt to obtain frankincense trees. Among the spices the Queen of Sheba, 500 years later brought as gifts to Solomon were the balsams he planted around Jericho. Historians say a garden of spices bloomed in Marit, the Queen of Sheba's capitol. The ancients knew the aloe can cure. The juice heals burns and mixes with honey for cough syrup. Boiled, the juice becomes a resin for laxatives and fever. Modern medicine adds to its uses in treating high blood pressure and ulcers. And the gel goes into sunburn lotions.

Nutmeg is not alone the spicy zest it gives to Granny's potato pudding. Oil extracted from the bark is narcotic and hallucinatory. It's one of the witch doctor's hallucinogens. I've heard the peyote cactus grows in the island's more arid spots. A button from this plant, when chewed, contains also a certain hallucinogen that the bocor uses himself to make contact with the loas.

"Does the witch doctor use only drugs that depress or stimulate?" Chris was fascinated with the subject.

The most familiar to us is coffee. The berries contain only one percent caffeine, but the bark and seeds as much as six percent. The Indians of Brazil mixed the coffee bark extract with cassava for an energizer in the rubber and diamond booms in the Amazon region. Your lignum vitae, snake root and black Indian hemp are most likely growing in witch doctors' gardens. If you find strophantus, most deadly of them all, their forebears brought it from Africa. The seeds or roots of the bush are pulverized and boiled and the syrup applied to the spears of elephant hunters along the Ivory Coast.

The poison is known to remain potent for as long as thirty years. It may be found in the forest as a climber with funnel-shaped whitish flowers with purple throats and cucumber-like fruit.

Another plant that is somewhat similar in its effect on the heart and is a paralysant of the nerve endings is curare. This is the arrow poison of the South American Indians. A closely guarded secret no white man would be permitted to watch, the bark is stripped off the large vines and pounded. This they put into rolled plantain leaves to make funnels through which they pour water. The yellow juice thus extracted is reduced by evaporation and may be added to cassava to make it adhere to an arrow. Death occurs in five to twenty five minutes. It can kill so quietly the victim will not know whence the poison came. Curare is more likely the witch doctor's choice, despite the deadly strophantus, which has been known to kill an enemy who was clawed by a fingernail dipped in the poison. The curare pot may get a few poisonous ants and some snake venom added to increase its potency. But here we have fact and what seems magic blessing and bane fruit of the same vine. In the past decade this killer has been re-embodied by medical research into a life keeper. It relaxes muscles before shock treatment in mental disease and before surgical procedures and in reducing fractures.

"Wasn't there a Canadian psychiatrist who went off to Liberia and got a sample of a witch doctor's magic compound for treating mental illness? He found that he boiled the root of Rauwolfia trees, and used the tea for about everything. A little was equal to a few drops of paregoric in soothing a sick baby. It became a tranquilizer when evil spirits plagued or when cataracts were removed. It served as an antidote for snakebite. It came in handy even in fever and vomiting and headache," added Sandy.

"True," the doctor confirmed. "One object of my botanical survey on this island is to seek for other species of the Rauwolfia tree. One variety grows on some of these Caribbean Islands, but its roots may not produce the derivative, reserpine, which the pharmacologists seek. But it is increasingly difficult for me to take off on a trek." Turning to Wallace, he added, "Setting up our trip into the north will hinge on our getting more help at Schweitzer soon. We saw over two hundred patients yesterday."

"We're in the same bind. Dr. Pressoir is still ill. We saw one hundred and twenty some at the outpatient clinic today. Slim chance for me to find time for a field trip until he returns. We must make a visit to the people over in the northwest. They are suffering from drought. Perhaps one of the boys..." Wallace held out

"Wait until I am back in August," suggested Sandy. "I'll be in materia medica next quarter, and hopefully will know my way among botanicals. Doctor, you haven't mentioned datura. In this plant family, medicine has found some helpful surprises—the truth serum, twilight sleep, others?"

True. The nightshades. Shakespeare's practitioners knew about them too. But we get atropine, an indispensable respiratory and circulatory stimulant. Another derivative relieves asthma. Another is used in obstetrics. Of course, the most familiar plant of the species is ornery Jimpson weed. Some species were found growing around ancient Inca temple operating rooms, thought to have been used in the surgery of the priests. A patient could be put into a coma for several days. But there's another ornamental tree found in the witch doctor's garden, the culebra, which is also in the datura family. In fact, it's "his" tree. The leaves are gathered on the waning of the moon and a fresh infusion from them is violently hallucinating. Of course, the village is asleep when he does his collecting. He may make a soothing poultice to reduce swelling or relieve pain. It's balmy in the bath. But when he mixes an unguent of belladonna, henbane and datura, and rubs it on the forehead of a patient, he produces a twenty four hour sleep, ridden by frenzy and terror, even delirium. In such dispatches he discovers secrets—stolen articles, hexes, and enemy's wiles, the victor in a cockfight. He even gives himself up to delirium to enable him to communicate with the spirits. Datura is put into rum for the ceremonial orgies.

"What does he do for an antidote when his decoction is too potent?" queried Sandy.

His formulary wouldn't be complete without antidotes. His failures are tragic, for all his practice is based on trial and error. He will use calabar bean (physostigmine) for curare. Tree barks that contain tannin for strophantus (ouabain). But he uses a part of the ouabain plant to treat syphilis, and we go to it for cortisone. He uses dried corn silks or Indian poke to counteract an overdose of heart stimulant. He's long on hallucinogens. One peyote (cactus) bean can produce loss of muscular coordination and exhilaration followed by vivid hallucinations in swirling colors. Shakespeare's witch knew her formula when she tossed in the toe of a frog. One of our most potent hallucinogens, bufotenin, comes from frog skin. It's just another case of seeing science and black magic, truth and superstition, walking side by side.

"And it matters not who is the practitioner," supplied Granny. "There's a handle to every mind, doctor. It's our aim to get hold of it. We study the best avenue to their hearts, and when the witch doctor himself becomes convinced that he is helplessly under the power of evil and can be emancipated from his bondage, we see another miracle of God's grace. Janoi makes thirty witch doctors, all told, who have found new fullness of life. And all yearn to learn. Antoine went to the kombit with all the

neighbors to help Jules ready his field for planting. But when the work was done, and the others stayed to make merry and dance, Antoine came home, and on down to my house to the readers' class. He wants to read the Word. He was as happy as a child when he could say his first words in the primer," she chuckled.

Mrs. Jamieson had been helping Granny fold some clean rags for the hospital. "I take care of a rag as I do my clothes," Granny said, collecting the stack. "We are going on. You have your key. We'll see you for breakfast." Granny's day had been long enough.

"Now that Granny has left us to our excesses," began David, filling the tiny coffee cups, "the Haitian bows to his own dim light and says, 'Tout sa ou pa konnen pi gran pase ou' (All that you do not know is greater than you); now pray tell us how come zombies?"

" 'Jan shashe, Jan twouve, Jan anbarase.' (John seeks, John finds, John is embarrassed.) It fits too well to pass up," apologized their guest. "Well, there is still another—'Twop lespri, sot pa lwen' (Genius is akin to madness) that explains how they pin the blame where it belongs. With no moral governor on his license to experiment, the unscrupulous rides roughshod where angels and science fear to tread. If we could observe the witch doctor produce that deep sleep that simulates death, and with time and place well in hand, we might see him succeed in bringing the patient back. Who of us would deny irreversible arrest of brain function? Tales of persons buried, then exhumed and recognized living as mindless slaves, called zombies, have basis. A society such as ours that sees the abuse of LSD, lycergine, the barbiturates, and harder drugs as commonplace, could scarcely reject it as a shocking possibility. The Haitian has another ready for us here, 'Pa bliye gra chemen pou cheme travès' (Do not let the crossroads let you forget the high road)."

A clock somewhere indicated the lateness of the hour. "Granny has the best solution of all," insisted Dr. Jamieson. "Education and better government will come. But conversion of thirty of these practitioners of the dark arts, that's the miracle of progress to toast! Here's to the noblest spirit in Haiti!" And he rose to say good night.

When the others had gone to their rooms, and the house settled for the night, Wallace helped Eleanor draw the simple, handwoven draperies. Both noted a less brilliant moon. "Pray that the dry season will end soon. We're on that last reservoir—the small one," said Wallace. And Eleanor knew the meaning!

Coral Reefs

Such a sensory excursion is
crystallized forever in memory's garden.

Eleanor was in the storeroom, going through a batch of bathing suits. It was a perfect day to take the trip out to the coral reefs and one of her guests needed a bathing suit. Everything in the storeroom had been carefully sorted as it came out of the missionary barrels. A bunch of corsets with stays might have been around longest. "Betty is a little imaginative genius. These stays are sure to transmigrate to hoops for little Creole dolls. Betty has a model about ready... One of these suits should fit you. Try on the blue one first. I'll join you as soon as I collect the outgoing mail, my shopping list, a basket of strawberries for the colonel's wife and another for Mrs. Mangones, and tell Dieula about lunch and dinner." Eleanor was walking as she talked and was now already in the house giving instructions for the day. Her guest and the two students would go down with Wally to the harbor.

The coral Iroquois reefs are about two miles from shore, shimmering in the turquoise waters of the bay. Made famous by William Beebe, and a lodestone for holiday makers who take the glass bottomed boats each morning, relatively few tourists have discovered these reefs and coves. The sea and sun preserve the island's perpetual summer and the bay's tranquillity. A Dutch freighter, too big to make it into harbor, rests at anchor; and a Chinese fishing boat bringing tuna for the cannery soon leaves us to float on an azure tide of star-spangled waves. Why are there not fleets of fishing boats? The Haitian, like his African forebears, shows little attraction to the sea. Truly, the sea about him might offer a ready solution to his food problem. But he lacks the capital and enterprise to invest in commercial fishing gear to harvest the teeming abundance of barracuda, tuna, sailfish and kingfish in the waters around his island.

The noonday sun glints on an expanse of fractured wave crests rolling in from the Caribbean. Our attention, however, is below the blue and crystal waters. We are now above the reefs, a garden of coral. This underwater realm is better visited by snorkeling. So we leave the boat and float in a ring of inflated inner tubes. Our shadows send schools of multihued fishes streaking for the depths—queen angelfish, squirrelfish, spadefish. One of the divers brings a breathtaking school of rainbow parrot swarming after the tempting sea urchin he lets slip through his fingers. As the snorkeler accustoms to the show below, he drifts lazily with face downward in the pellucid water, revels in the shimmering display of sea fan lace, sea plumes, turtle grass, crimson sponge, and staghorn coral. New swarms of rich hued tropical reef dwellers dart after the divers' morsels of sea urchin.

Coral is one of nature's most fantastic creations. Actually a living animal, it lives in all the oceans but forms reefs only in waters above 68 degrees. The coral is manufactured by little sea animals similar to jellyfish and sea anemones, called cnidarions. Rapidly multiplying colonies of polyps extract lime from sea water to create coral formations of infinite variety. These are hard as stone, yet live. Generation after generation of tiny animals add layer upon layer of fantasy, which now seemingly lies only an inch or so below the surface. This iridescent realm has been thousands of years actually building nearer and nearer the surface. The reefs above the water are lifeless.

Drawn into a timeless visit below, one drifts with the translucent interplay of waves, and dwells with the violet and saffron and honey fronds, the fairyland domes, the fans and stars, and sparkling stretches of sand, and even yearns to drop far below into the shadowless cobalt blue, there to discover yet unexplored coral species, sponges, sea whips, and the fascinating life within the grottoes of the deep.

Hurricanes

Of all who came, some saw and were touched. Others shrugged off the whole island as another hungry, hopeless, hapless, tortured mass of humanity too late to be salvaged. Some even ventured, "By most counts, Haiti's problems are terminal. Why do you stay?"

"Controlling the weather may be a dream of the meteorologists, but such an achievement could bring untold benefit to this part of the world," the engineer was saying. André had come up to visit the Turnbulls and talk with Wallace about laying telephone cable above Petionville. It was after the evening meal.

"Weather can be predicted. Why not controlled? Seeding a hurricane that is full-blown is not the way. Why not dissipate it while it is out there building up in the Atlantic?" offered Wally

"They bring much needed rain," his father began, "but these storms are becoming increasingly more destructive. Hazel killed two thousand on this island in 1954. She had thrashed around in the West Indies for a week, then crossed over Haiti on October 12. Haiti's 8,000-foot peaks weakened her, but two hundred more were killed in the Kenscoff area and seventy five buried in a landslide. Flora struck in October, too, in 1963. That storm was the worst killer in history—six thousand on this island and as many in Cuba. Then in the final days of September, 1966, Inez practically destroyed Jacmel. She writhed like a wounded serpent for eighteen days across the Atlantic, hit Haiti, then moved on to a dying thrust against Mexico's high mountains."

Wallace went on. "This part of the world is peculiarly vulnerable to this kind of storm. The Tainos, an aboriginal Arawakan tribe that lived in the Caribbean, called this dreadful angry wind that blew in and destroyed everything in its path, Hurakan, their name for an evil spirit. Other tribes of Central and South America's northern coast had similar names for their thunder and lightning god. It was not a hurricane, however, that broke up the Santa Maria on a reef in 1492. Her draft was unsuited to nosing around reefs and in shallow island waters. Columbus declared the weather was like May on that first voyage. It was two voyages later, the Spanish explorers having loaded twenty ships with the gold of the Incas, and against Columbus' advice, set their flotilla in the path of a building hurricane. All but Columbus' own ship sank in that deepest point in the Atlantic Ocean, Mona Passage, between Puerto Rico and Hispaniola, carrying five hundred men and their ships 300 fathoms deep. That trench is about five miles deep. On his last voyage he met another hurricane which he battled nine days, before his ship was cast up on the northern coast of Jamaica. He didn't make his final return to Spain until 1504, the year Queen Isabella died."

"Great indeed were Columbus' successes as a mariner in the light of today's knowledge," agreed the engineer.

The Engineer Explains

These storms are formed in a quiet span of ocean between the trade wind belts, called The Doldrums. The trade winds sweep downward across the equator off the west coast of Africa, outward into the Atlantic following the earth's rotation, then upward back across the equator along the eastern U.S. coast line all the way to Newfoundland. They contour their circuit back by the British Isles. Sailing vessels charted these winds. The sail ship routes from Liverpool to South Africa and those from New York to the Cape of Good Hope formed a parallel course across this expanse of the Atlantic. A sailing vessel might note on its log that it passed through a shower but the air remained hot and oppressive. A TWA jet might encounter a stretch of bumpy atmosphere. Each might have nudged the incubator of a new storm.

For several days a shunt of air swings up and back over an overheated spot on the Atlantic's equatorial belt. This hot moist air moves indifferently until it bumps into something, maybe a rocky knoll of one of the Verdes lying farthest from the ample rump of west Africa. Not strong enough to sweep over the knoll, it separates, then comes back together as an eddy, warmed and condensed into a drizzle, warmed and condensed, feeding itself warm lower air and cool upper air until there is a cycle of breeze and shower. A steamer encountering this cycle might have its decks smothered in soot from its own smokestack and the ship's log note a few minutes later, "Ship rolling. Barometer falling. Spray from stern to stern. Storm making up."

This front picks up momentum as it also picks up tons of moisture and its winds accelerate with each cycle around a wider and wider center. In the Atlantic it's called a hurricane. In the Pacific, a typhoon.

The earth's rotation deflects winds of the northern hemisphere to the right, of the southern hemisphere, to the left. In the Atlantic the force spins counterclockwise. There are other explanations of how a storm is born. Some believe the earth's rotation at the equator, which is a thousand miles an hour, starts a pattern of warm air lifting, moving, cooling, condensing. This increasing pattern builds up a force greater than a nuclear bomb. With nothing to stop it, this rotation may grow with a vortex over three or four hundred miles, and travel a couple of thousand miles, always northwesterly.

Hurricane Hazel

The Turnbulls and Granny were thinking of Hazel in 1954. There were no weather forecasts or means of warning the people. There had been an especially long drought. Sunday morning the congregation, poor always but suffering now and fearful because the grass had withered and the millet curled inward, had prayed for rain. "Send rain, O Lord, we pray," pled Soimeus, the Fermathe pastor, and all the flock intoned, "Rain, O Lord!" The mountains lay golden brown save for an occasional narrow band of green edging a lessening spring far below. All the day before and Sunday the atmosphere had been unusually clear. It seemed to be a sign. Every drought at long last comes to an end. Rain was coming. The south wind which had been a gentle breeze all day was steadily growing a little stronger. For several nights the Voodoo drums had throbbed until dawn. The spirits were angry.

Two college students, helping for a semester at the mission, had gone down to the bay to go sailing. The far reaches of the bay lay blue and quiet in the sunshine, with just enough breeze to fill their sails. There were dozens of other craft out—yawls and ketches, expensive cabin cruisers, fishing craft, small sailboats like the one the boys chose.

Camions and cars clattered and rumbled through clouds of yellow dust on the roads. Some of the people were at work on their roofs against the onslaught of the coming rainy season. Then, suddenly, it was dusk, the dust suspended in veils in the glancing glare and shadow of headlights. The dryness and smell of dust stung the nostrils of women and children hurrying along the roads and trails. Rain, life giving rain would soon be reviving seer and dried vegetation. Seeds would sprout. There would be corn to wait to mature, and beans. With the promise of rain to revive their parched land, fill reservoirs and rivers, turn the leaves of the orange trees dark, liven the branches of the mango, turn the slopes green, the villagers rejoiced that man and beast would revel together in the freshet.

Veteran mariners look to double mooring, fearful of hurricane.

Wallace Remembers

Our falling barometer had warned us for hours. It is all still so vivid. Twice the roof had been blown off our still unfinished house, so I had taken extra precaution. But as the sky darkened and the winds rose for two days, October 10 and 11, our apprehensions grew. We had no radio warnings or way of tracing the storm then. Deciding that it might be bad, on the eleventh I sent runners for the farmers to get in their animals. They would place livestock downwind on the slopes where they would picket them, and keep smaller animals in their huts with them. The boys had come back with reports of veteran seamen looking to doubled mooring. The witch doctor had tossed ashes on water in a gourd, and had sent out word for the people to go to the caves.

The church, our houses, the hospital, had no glass windows, only wooden shutters which we locked own with long iron hooks. One part of our house lacked shutters, so we had barred the openings with sheets of metal roofing, wedged in place by heavy timbers supported by foot-round rocks.

Eleanor Takes Up

It was about four in the afternoon. The sky was black with rain-pregnant clouds. Coming in on the Dominican Republic side of the island, the mighty force of tropical air rode upward when it reached the southern slopes of La Selle, and the downfall of rain was horrendous. The rain would drive with gale force, then seem to turn back on itself, then rush ahead again, rising and driving.

I thought I would dash across the yard to Granny's house, but outside, suddenly as if a gigantic prow was moving water and wind the air was drawn from my lungs and my feet deserted me. Summoning all my strength I clung to the door frame and clawed my way inside. Wallace was calling for help to hold down the timbers heaving against the sheets of metal. For somewhere near an hour we held and rode up and down up and down as the wind heaved against them. Then there was a sudden lull.

I left my post and dashed out again to see about Granny and the children. Trees lay across my path, banana, coffee and oleander stripped of their leaves, palms bent to the ground the rabbit pens a shambles, the goat pen rubble. Everything was under a scramble of limbs and leaves and debris. And overhead strange tropical birds were flying about wildly. The roar of the wind had ceased. A patch of blue sky appeared overhead. The rain had stopped, and the air was hot and oppressive. The average eye of a hurricane is fourteen miles. Hazel's was much greater, or I would never have made it over to Granny's and back again. But I recall how ominous was the quiet. The relaxed sensation of sound was itself deafening. Suddenly, as I climbed back over the flamboyant branches across our doorstep, a crashing onslaught of rain and wind bore down upon me, hurling me groping against the door. Wallace pulled me inside and we ran again to our station with the timbers. Massive blasts of wind threatened to take the whole house. Our fears were for the hundreds of people about us in their little thatched huts, huddling and shivering. How could they escape the savage destruction of a wind so mighty?

At last, after what seemed hours of relentless thudding in the darkness, a faint light seemed to transfuse the gray-black night. The rain, still torrential, seemed to have less roar. But there was no letup all night, all the next day, and the next five days of it.

Eleanor's voice betrayed the iron that entered the soul!

Granny and the Boys

Granny's mind was still back in that fateful time. The three little grandsons were over at her house. They had been with her through it all. Now it was early afternoon and the lamp was on for the fifth day of crashing downpour. "Once there was a mama who had three little boys... one with hair like marmalade and one with hair like honey., TiWally's was the marmalade and Sandy's was the honey. Baby David would ask, "What is mine Granny?" "Like brown sugar, son, when the cane is cooked down to candy." All three boys knew about sugarcane, had watched the oxen lumber out of the canefields, and had even ridden on top of the high stacks to the huge refinery. A juicy section of cane was always a treat to mountain boys. The cane is grown only in the coast al lowlands. More special still was the juice boiled down to make cane candy, which Granny had saved for a rainy day. Granny was good at making up stories to lessen the little boys fret at so long a stay inside. But she never dreamed any rainy day, let alone five in a row, could be like this. The storm had hurled the water with so great force against her thick stone walls, it had been an unending struggle to mop the water and to keep a small fire burning.

Wallace and Rescue Team

As soon as the rains slacked, we went outside to a world of incredible ruin. The fissures in our dry earth had widened to gullies that carried the water across the yard, the garden, the play yard, in torrents down the mountainside. All our roofs had channeled gushes of water into the reservoirs. The fish pond overflowed and met water pouring from the basement of Granny's house. Water was leaping from drainways, down new-formed riddles of troughing, baring rocks and tree roots and carrying topsoil and debris to the ravines below.

It continued to rain for three or four days longer. After an inspection of the mission community, we believed the plight of the flooded areas below more critical. Soon there were neighboring villagers on our porch telling of homes gone, children pinned under the poles that held the thatch, mud and stone walls crumbling in on a family, pots and gourds becoming flying missiles that bashed heads, splinters driven through arms, people lost on the trails or blown away, animals dead.

As the day wore on, the crowd grew. The church, the hostel, our porches became temporary shelter for cold, wet and hungry women and children. Some of the men were searching for precious pieces of tin, cutting the ruined banana stalks for animal food, and helping clear the mission road so we could get the jeep out. In boots and slickers we made it up to Kenscoff, trees, roofs, tangled debris obscuring almost every foot of the nicked, chewed, gutted and eroded road. The tall pines, which had made Kenscoff the mountain resort for many from the city, littered the area so heavily the road was totally obstructed, as if a maddened giant had slashed and battered and twisted them until they were all felled. Leaving the jeep, we reached the police post, to find the mountain people beginning to come for help, wet, cold, and homeless. The police had no radio contact beyond and could tell us no more than we could see.

When we got back to the mission it was dark, still raining, and Granny was setting up a refugee camp. After a sleepless night, the rain still falling, we knew waters were still rising in the lowlands where hazard for life was bound to be greater than in the mountain regions. Leaving Granny to "man" the mission, we set out the next morning for Port-au-Prince. Only three months before this, Dr. Roy a noted physician, had organized a Red Cross charter. We were among the fifty charter members. Despite trees, boulders, deep cuts, mud deposits and slides, we got to the city and found Dr. Roy, to report our situation and to offer our help. All communication out, the city was just beginning to comprehend the magnitude of the disaster. Dr. Roy instructed us to take a supply of first aid emergency supplies back to the mission, collect some things for rescue work and set out with a doctor and sanitary officer as soon as we could return. By the time we had made the trek back up the mountain, told Granny we might be out several days, and set out a second time for Port-au-Prince, we were met at the mission entrance by Catule, breathless with news he had heard from a man from Bongar. A slide had sloughed off a mountain face taking at least twenty five families into the gorge below. The people of Bongar could look across at daybreak and see the awful raw mountainside. We knew the Artibonite, the Trois Riviéres, the Froide, the Limbé, the Grise, the Grande, and the Gros Morne, every river and its tributary on the island was surging in tumult over its banks. Erstwhile dry sand beds all, they now boiled and foamed over rocks and boulders and cascaded in waterfalls over ledges and rushed through ravines now flooding. We knew that the rice and cotton, citrus and hemp in the lowlands as well as the coffee and grain and vegetables in the mountains were washed away or buried under layers of mud.

To see about the little flock at Dumay, I crossed the widened, still roaring Grise, stripped to shorts and helmet, which the current tried to take. A hungry and homeless, but safe, group gathered around me. They had spent the worst days in the shelter of the mission church, which stood. I turned to the disaster compounded on the mountain, later directing the helicopters to drop them food.

When we reported the landslide to Dr. Roy, we spent the rest of the day preparing to load two horses with supplies and guide a relief team into the landslide area. He provided us with forty yards of white cloth to use in signaling if the weather should clear enough to permit an army plane or helicopter to fly in. We left as soon as it was light the next morning, beginning the ascent over slippery trails, often clinging perilously to the muddy mountain face for footing. Before midday, after unsaddling and unloading the two ponies several times to span a cut in the trail, we saw it would be impossible for them to make the climb, so we turned them back, continuing with the heavier equipment and two porters. We kept only the forty yards of cloth, our bedding and a bag of food. The rain never stopped falling and the deafening roar from the ravines underscored the perils of our undertaking. We trudged and struggled until near nightfall, when we found ourselves across the raging Momance near a hut, where the six of us sought shelter for the night. We soon learned that our host was a witch doctor but his array of charms and fetishes had no power to discourage sleep, nor did the stench of animals he had retrieved from the river below. The Haitian gets his salt from sea salt which he brings up from the fish market. The witch doctor had been unable to provide a dry place, let alone enough salt nor could he get his wood to burn under his pot. The Haitian's taste for meat is so great that he is not overly concerned about the state of preservation. His stomach with a cast iron lining can withstand what to us would be a violent gastronomic insult, and get by with it. Lacking refrigeration, he resorts to drying or smoking. Under the circumstances we felt sorry that he would be denied even one meal by either process. One gets used to the smells of these one-room huts with cold, damp, dirt floors, pots and gourds hanging overhead. Sometimes a dog or cat or chickens refuse to move out, and we couldn't expect them to on a night like that.

With one roving trespasser we were unprepared to share our refuge. Our provisions close by, in the night we were awakened by a light shuffling which we suspected was a thief after our rice and beans. In another instant we made out the form of a boa constrictor on his way to the wall in pursuit of a rat. The sound he made was like a big rope being dragged across the crude floor.

The second night we slept in the hut of a Christian family. The next morning we heard the army plane overhead, but clouds obscured it. To signal would be useless. We continued our climb, the trail narrowing to only a few inches at times between us and a sheer drop of hundreds of feet to the gorge below. There were fallen rocks to be inched around and water undermining every foot of the trail.

"And," Wallace interrupted himself, "my personal tribulation compounded when I discovered that the soles of my bare feet had become embedded with slivers of sharp gravely sand when we crossed the Grise."

Mountain Slide

The mountain people's very struggle for existence had favored the monstrous treachery which rode with this storm, and the one in 1964, and again in 1966. They had cut their trees down to make charcoal for fuel and to sell in the market. Even when the government passed a law forbidding them to cut down a living tree, it was common practice to ring the bark to make the tree die. The tree was dead. And no seedling replaced it. Erosion was already a recognized national problem, even back then. To prevent wastage of topsoil and limestone, the chief allies of the mountains are the trees. They bind the soil with their roots as with tough sisal and weld the earth with the grass and leaves. Burrowers insects, rodents and worms work up the earth that rains wash away. And grazers. They are the real troublemakers. They eat the cover of grass and leaves and their sharp hooves wear trails that running water cuts into gullies.

Now, on that fateful night across from Bongar, so much of the rim above the Froide gorge had been robbed of its small brush, the rains cut a deep gulch. Assaulted by the deluge, crevices lost all their deposits of sand and loam, and allowed a deep cut to carry away all the earth around a huge rock outcropping. The shelf shifted slightly, and this small movement of the foundation let loose the whole mass. With one horrendous roar a million tons of rim plunged down hundreds of feet before it was halted by trees, then slid with the trees, rock walls and small growth on down several hundred more feet to block the gorge, now a crashing, rampant river. Nothing down the mountainside was left—twenty five families, their houses and huts and everything was buried in one gigantic mass, still moving with the earth's pull downward like molten lava. Only the wide, bare, raw gravel and rock gaped the story of ineffable tragedy. All the neighboring farmers were so stunned, they still sat inside their wattle houses and stared or moaned. Almost everyone had lost close relatives. And each survivor had his own tale of terror and loss.

Pierrezine, alone of the Barriére Roche community, survived of all those in the path of the slide. Living in the valley, and having borne the local witch doctor two children, she declared a white-clad figure appeared in her hut and spoke a message of warning that the people were going to be destroyed. Holding banana leaves over her head in the drenching rain, she went to every hut in the valley and gave the message, then climbed the mountain to her daughter, who gave birth that night.

Jacques was squatting before his kitchen fire when his hut was swept away. A boulder hit him from behind like a billiard ball and shot him twenty feet out of the path of the slide.

Jété was standing in the water with her mother when their hut was taken, the wattles scoring her back as she was flattened beneath it. She pulled her leg out of the ground and ran out of the valley.

Aristil's family, the valley's only Christians had gone over the mountain to plant corn leaving him a teenager to watch the hut and tend the pigs. He alone perished of the large household.

Hermann and his neighbors saw, in the lightning flashes, that the mountain was sliding. His friend and he held the door, to keep it from being pushed in with the wind. He was a Christian and neighbors had flocked to his house.

Another heard a great roar above his hut. Terrified in the darkness and rain, he dragged one child and his wife outside and across the potato rows, as dimly he saw a clump of trees riding downward. Then the slide thundered past. His hut held for a moment, then moved with the whole shelf on which it stood.

As the rains continued, surface mud and limestone turned loose, undermining peripheral huts and carrying them down, too. The gorge, outrageously choked with debris and mud and trees, heaved and thundered and broke loose again and again, a hurtling cascade. And this raging, churning mass surged on down, finally to fill the harbor with more silt. Limestone and gravel stretched a mile or more across the gorge, here fifty, there a hundred feet deep in wasteland. In such a disaster there are those spared, people not needing to be taken to a hospital, but people needing food, fuel, blankets, and encouragement to begin again.

Our third day out we saw a helicopter through the mist and clouds. Fortunately we had camped on the only level spot on the mountain. So we opened our cloth code. The chopper saw it and landed. They brought supplies and took out news. A witch doctor's peristyle, an open straw-roofed pavilion enclosed by a lattice fence to keep out pigs and dogs, was our guest chamber that last night. The next day the helicopter picked us up and dropped us in Port-au-Prince in twenty minutes. It had taken us thirty six hours on foot.

Back at the mission we found Granny running a soup kitchen for more than sixty homeless in our immediate area. We knew the suffering had only begun. The weeks and months that followed, strenuous and exhausting, plunged us into a desperate struggle for survival for thousands of Haitians. We were to see many die, and extremity come to all.

Flora and Inez

The island was spared nine years, then Flora struck in October also and next, Inez. It had never recovered in many respects from the first storm. The rural farmers continued in their old ways of doing things. Flora was a repeat performance for the mountains, and still worse for the plains. Eleanor was a guide on the helicopters getting food and medical supplies to the stricken areas. Sandy was also guiding on one that got caught in a downdraft. The crew jettisoned the bags of supplies and almost struck the side of the mountain, breaking off the back wheel and damaging the blades as the chopper sliced through the limbs of a mango tree. The crippled chopper churned and wobbled back to base on a miracle of skill and providence with a big branch stuck in its side. The pilot met Eleanor's concern with, "Lady, it's the closest I ever want to come to not coming back. These are magnesium and burn in five minutes!" His chopper did not fly any more missions in Haiti!

That was also the time Mrs. Mellon came up from Deschappelles to help Granny and run an ambulance to Port-au-Prince hospitals. She helped care for the children, washing filthy clothes, cooking.

The hurricane that devastated Jacmel was the disaster most of the outside world heard about. This was hurricane Inez which also did two million dollars, damage to Port-au-Prince.

There was concern in the States for the island. The U.S. government had broken off diplomatic negotiations with Haiti in disapproval of the Duvalier regime. But when the report went out that four thousand had died—actually the figures were conservative, for there was no way to determine how many had died—the United States did send help.

As twice before, Wallace was made director of the relief operation in the Kenscoff area. Jacmel is just over the mountains from Kenscoff on the map, but the road the U.S. Marines hacked out six thousand feet up stopped short of connecting these two points. In 1915 when the Marines quelled the mob that had dismembered Guillaume Sam, they never knew how long and well their muscle and brawn road would serve, nor how well a few more miles of hacking would have burnished their memory. Jacmel, idyllic little palm shaded paradise, was changed from tranquil existence to incredibly horrible tragedy. For days a raging tempest had washed and lashed, plunging waves twenty feet high inland. A hurricane tide is a churning maelstrom which topples docks and piers and carries the wrecked timbers inland to pound to pieces everything in its path. As if maddened by convulsions of its unfathomed deeps, the sea had hurled thousands of tons of water inland, then sucked it all out again. Mud huts with people and animals and vehicles swirled on the tide like leaves. Human beings who escaped clung desperately to anything left standing—mango trees, palms, rocky crags. Too often death awaited because these havens offered no protection from continuing rain, hunger, and pneumonia.

When help arrived with the first relief detachment, the storm had passed, but the skies remained unsettled, brooding with clouds. All that had been the quaint town of Jacmel a few days before was now desolation and tangled wreckage. Stinking mud, bloated human and animal bodies lay everywhere along the coast. In some places twenty to fifty bodies had worked together like driftwood. Survivors struggled, dazed, through the muck, searching for loved ones. Hapless fathers sought children who had been swept from their arms into the swirling flood. Roads were gouged, great chasms yawned in streets. Dazed survivors roamed about, digging into the rubble for any kind of food. The whole area exuded a sickly sweet stench. With all the decomposition of bodies, there would be grave health problems.

Teams set to work with DDT and gasoline to reduce epidemic hazards. A U.S. helicopter began plying back and forth between the carrier Boxer and the shore, delivering food and medical supplies. Not a building stood intact in which a canteen or dispensary could be set up. To combat the fetid smell of death and decay, a corps of workers began burying the dead in mass graves; too slow and impractical, the bodies had to be piled in heaps and burned. The heat made the task formidable beyond description. Hundreds of bodies had been washed out to sea, making any accurate death count impossible. As one detail moved in with food and drinking water, another set up first aid. Then several work crews began the all important task of clearing debris, filling craters and washed out roadbeds to restore temporary traffic.

After the emergency phase, followed the long, exhausting one-step-forward-another-backward fatigue duty of rehabilitation. It was months before most of the island could move from stark, harsh, and desolating survival to so much as a toehold on self-sustainment.

Two hurricanes followed by six months of drought. Two seasons with no crops. Two and one half years of hunger and starvation, TB rampant! Memories haunt even yet... "We put our seed in the ground three times. The field was as it was the first time..."

A woman lay on the dirt floor, emaciated, lifeless. "It began with a hurting in her stomach. She turned yellow like a ripe mango. No blood in her."

Three fell to their death while trying to make a garden on the steep slopes, too weak to grip with their toes.

The ragged and barefoot Christians who came to church, eyes sunken and faces drawn, still sang with single-handed fervor, I'd Rather Have Jesus.

Shrunken and weak, Albert came, his hair turned red, as had the hair of many others, from protein deficiency. "Since six days we haven't melted the salt in the water." With no food to cook, he and his children put the sea salt under their tongues to lessen the hunger pangs. Pray, couldn't he do some work for a little food?

A young father of two small children begged for a little flour to make a gruel. He had been to everyone he knew to borrow two dollars with which to buy boards to make a coffin for his wife who had died of starvation.

Their seed had been washed away. Too late to plant corn. No prospect of a crop this season. Famished children would steal into the scant potato patch planted with yam ends, or the sparse corn plot, grovel with their hands and filch the young sprouts.

A little six year old brought to the hospital died soon after arrival. Another and another and another.

What is malnutrition? Dr. Mellon says it's a fancy word for slow starvation. If you could see the gaunt forms huddled every morning in the mission front yard begging for work... They can tell you...

It's a mud hut with thatched roof, home to perhaps nine to fourteen, the youngest a baby, the oldest threescore and ten, a skin and bones pig staked to the guava tree at the door. In the morning some coffee. Nothing more until evening. Maybe nothing more for another day or so. Bare feet move less agilely down the slope to the spring. Each gourdful marks the struggle for survival another day. The water flows less abundantly. Today will be a little drier. The sun will be a little hotter. The few goats and dogs don't have enough water. The baked earth sears bare feet. The scrub rattles like dry paper. The heat shimmers, blinding. The green of the land has changed to rust. Down below, the streams that yesterday came muddy to the waist today slosh clear water at the ankles. The women are out in the deepest part washing their clothes.

"No ship is available to bring our December shipment of U.S. surplus food. So many are dying..." Granny wrote.

Later: "How great a blessing the food that comes through CARE. The U.S. churches which designate twenty five dollars a month for Haiti are our lifeline for corn meal, cracked wheat, milk, flour, and beans in 50 and 100-pound bags, and cooking oil in cases. The people beg daily to do work for food. We let them work one week in relays in order to give more families a chance to have food.

"TB is rampant all over the island. Some of the missionaries in the lowlands have come down with it, and have come up to Fermathe for rest, fresh air, and food. Wallace and the work gang and two visitors from Minnesota kept going into the night to get the roof on the TB shelter. This will be the rest house for these patients and their relatives, closer to the hospital for treatment and no longer below us with their vermin." The original three rooms had grown to eight across the mountain face, with rooms below for cooking and laundry and hostelry.

All work and workers required supervision. Food had to be prepared for the sick and their relatives, for Stateside visitors, and many who just sought a rest stop. There was an increasing stream of geologists, developers, government officials, roving journalists and just tourists. Step-by-step the house had grown above and on the shelf below to meet the growing needs of the only center of the compound administration and hospitality.

So great grew the suffering that the Christians began praying, "Lord Jesus, come quickly."

After the Storm

And there was Janoi...

All somehow knew there would be another harvest season, and Haiti's rural silos would again appear. The farmer would again tie his grain in bundles, climb with it up the palm closest to him, and anchor these clusters safely amid the topmost fronds. This ingenious storage system puts his corn and millet beyond the reach of animals and rodents.

Down in the lowlands the sugarcane harvest would revive again another ancient activity. Harvested by hand with machetes as it has been done since the 1700's, the sugarcane is loaded on ox-drawn carts, hauled to the sugar mill, where the only difference now is some modern machinery turning the cane into sugar, molasses, rum and alcohol. As the cane is crushed between huge iron rollers, its juice runs down a trough into a cauldron where it is cooked or drained into a fermenting vat to begin the distilling process. The crushed and stripped stalks are piled around the cauldron for fuel. As the syrup cooks down, the top is drained off as molasses, leaving the raw sugar to be scooped out of the bottom. And packed cane sugar treats would again be shared by children.

During those terrible weeks and months and years that followed the storms, Wally directed the relief. He distributed food, hundreds of pounds of vegetable seed, and in the spring, seed corn and beans, bringing courage and hope. All the main trails and roads in the mountain area, encompassing over 10,000 families, were reopened. Wally directed the work gangs.

The Haitian loves the kombit or work bee, which is a community project at harvest time. Neighbors and relatives join in reaping one farmer's crop, then move to another. The host may provide a pot of food and whatever liquid refreshment he can muster, and the musical entertainment. No other wages are expected. On the work bee pattern, homes were rebuilt, gardens and plots planted.

But most promising were the terracing bees. These involved six hundred households, many of them committed Christians. To begin, two hundred men would gather for a week's work on eroded farm plots. First, they hand plowed with picks, loosening limestone from the side of the mountain to build stone walls that would stop the erosion of the first plot. They learned to start with the largest stones, fit and stagger, then set. Thereafter the owner must carefully collect in a hollow anything that might decompose into compost. Contour rows were made to follow the slope, the scant soil disturbed as deeply as picks and hoes could penetrate, so nature could assist by rapidly disintegrating the exposed stony surface into soil. Hard on tools which must be replaced too often out of the family's meager earnings, the end result was neat and promising. Then the work gang would move to another plot.

The next week a second force of two hundred men would learn and prepare like the first; and the following week would take on the last two hundred. The rotation would bring the first two hundred back into the work cycle often enough to sustain their starving families. On Saturday the wage distribution was food.

Not all survived within the favored six hundred, so great was the suffering. None was untouched. One morning twelve year old David, out early shooting doves with his pellet gun, heard a whimpering. He had almost stumbled over a child shivering on the trail. In child to child language David learned that the little fellow's mother had abandoned him. Dirty and verminous, his shirt in shreds, David took him home, where he was scrubbed, his head shaved, two long, sharp thorns removed from his feet, then clothed and fed. When asked what he had eaten, startled and defensive, he cried, "No, my hand hasn't been put to my mouth in two days!"

When the planting season ended, and weeks of waiting finally produced a harvest, Christians thronged their little churches. Young David was up at dawn to go with the family to Bongar, two hours on horseback even after leaving the jeep road, for a thanksgiving service. No doubt about the genuineness of these Christians. They had brought cane, millet, pumpkins, corn, vegetables, and fruits, and piled them in front of the pulpit as symbolic thank offerings. Then, as part of the year's harvest, converts of the past twelve months came and stood, too.

Citing Blessings

Actually, more than 40,000 first generation believers were crowding over one hundred mission churches over the island. How different, how blessed, was the work with this new generation...

Like Calebasse, after bumping over a hand-hewn road by jeep, where five hundred gathered for a special service of thanksgiving because they worshipped now in a stone building with concrete floor and simple benches, and with upstanding promising TiPaul as their preacher. So short a time, mused Granny, since TiPaul was a lad in shirt and no pants (boys put on pants when they reach their ninth birthday) but found the Lord, and thereafter was fired with a tremendous desire for learning. His incessant questioning was return enough for the extra hours spent in teaching him. For TiPaul caught, as few had, the vital spirit of the Christian message.

Or like poor steeped-in-the-dust-and-ignorance Thomazeau, only forty miles by jeep, but as dark a hole as one could find; home of notorious Sauveur (savior), the witch doctor. Half the mission's TB patients had come from this area. Now, the slow agony of teaching them had yielded a cooperative spirit which was inspiring them to dig wells and irrigate their little plots for food.

Or like Drouin, thickly populated river area, with a growing group happily carrying hard to find building materials on their heads long distances in the hot sun, to build their church.

Or like Atrèl, where only fourteen believers have grown to five hundred, and this mother church sponsors five branches in the remote bush country of the northwest. Always one saint with more light and joy than the rest, there was Seda, an old blind Bible woman, who had prayed with such power these miracles had come to pass.

Or like communion Sunday at the mission church Fermathe. To partake of the Lord's Supper with these Haitian believers is a meaningful moment in the missionary's life. They had come over muddy, slippery and dangerous trails, five hundred of them, barefooted until they reached the church yard where they scraped off the mud, then took their sandals or well-worn shoes from their heads and put them on their feet to enter the church. To the strains of Jesus Is All the World to Me from the old pump organ they sang and Catule prayed, and he and the other oldest member Frére Gil, both deacons, took the offering. Even at seventy five Catule still took his son with him out on the trails to read Scripture while he prayed and witnessed. Many of those who murmured fervent amens had been brought to the Lord by Frère Gil.

Or like the happy melee on the volleyball court, on Monday afternoon for Granny's weekly Bible story hour, then to play. Yesterday the Methodists from Michigan tossed balls for two hours.

Or like the mission's pride and joy, Fort Jacques School, the pilot experiment in modern teaching instead of the traditional rote system.

Or like the Family Planning Unit, close enough to the church to provide space for Sunday school rooms on Sunday, across from the hospital where it draws record turnouts of women for instruction in family planning. Eleanor had brought the first intrauterine contraceptive to Haiti and she believed in the project in all its facets, despite an occasional setback. More than nine hundred women had cooperated in having IUDs and things looked promising, two cardinal failures excepted, when two women presented twins! (Eleanor called the program Double or Nothing, until a woman was delivered of triplets.)

Or like that little pearl of promise and purpose, the Mountain Maid self-help project, that pays out several thousand dollars each month to hundreds of families who do metal work, weave, carve, sew and embroider handmade aprons, napkins, placemats, tablecloths, guest towels, bibs, shirts and jackets. Their work means a livelihood, money for their children to stay in school, and support for their church. Candle-making also provides work for recovered TB patients. The mission is a regular stop for tourists who love to take home these fine samples of Haitian talent. Wally, and Betty, his wife, direct all the self-help work.

Or like the Need. Oh, the overwhelming, clamoring, mortal need of more help. Five to six thousand children eager to learn are crowding schoolrooms faster than teachers can be trained or found. Teaching means supervising twenty five to five hundred pupils, organizing, selecting, training, translating, and instructing, while stopping fights, inspecting for itch and lice, opposing but never ending a multitude of troubles they bring with them. Thirty to thirty five thousand new believers are crowding little churches faster than pastors can be vouchsafed and schooled for leadership. If only there were a thousand like herself ready to say with Granny, "Lord, send me!"

They Learn to Walk in the Way

The January sky wrapped the church spire in vesper gold and silhouetted the undulating roof of the tearoom in night shadows creeping up the slopes. The day was ending and David and Wallace reached the Turnbull house as a full moon lifted over the mountains. They looked across the valley to the distant horizon in time to see the sky change from palest lavender to tones of rose and purple. Zenas was at the organ, the music flowing in and out as he turned the pages of old familiar hymns, then lively tunes. Just as a spinning wheel has an alive hum, this house hummed of all the sounds in it; of footsteps, voices, Chris reading Creole aloud in the living room; of water poured; of eggs beaten in a bowl; of Eleanor bargaining at the kitchen door; of Granny and Nevart gaily measuring lining for Betty's bassinet. Open on all sides to let the beauty in, the house seems to settle for the outdoors as adornment enough, with Haitian tile to cover all the floors. Its stone walls and tile floors can stand against the insects, the sun, and the rain. A house with amicable disposition and casual manners, its heart is the large family room with dining area convenient to the kitchen. Two linen chests, a hutch graced by a collection of eighteenth century French china, and several tall back Haitian chairs are right and necessary with the authentic dining table.

Dieula was holding each plate for Wallace to give a serving of meat.

"There's something peculiarly your own about a piece of furniture," he was explaining, "which was a tree you have felled, then a drawing on a sheet of paper, then a piece of smoothed timber you helped the workmen transform into a shining, flawless top." The long table was dexterously designed to extend for twelve or telescope for half as many.

"Wallace thought of it as our family table," Eleanor added. "He wanted a big family."

A cluster of rose hibiscus floated in the celedon bowl centering the table, beneath the flicker of a brass lamp overhead. All that was unlovely forgotten in the gentle evening and the closeness of family and friends, such a setting easily stirred memory and glib conversation. Withal, the mood of those around the table hesitated. Dieula stepped softly with the dinner plates and Jesula came precariously with the bowls, her eyes on those at the table and not on what she carried.

"To change them from within—to inaugurate a fundamental departure from those centuries of tradition, to imbue them with moral direction, is to lead them out of animism into an enlightened way of life," Wallace began. "This must happen in their lives before they can be educated, or taught to conserve their soil and trees and grow more food to eat."

"Who can estimate the mental anguish and agony of spirit lifted from their hearts when they come to believe in a loving goodly Providence, that God is love and not mean and spiteful?" Eleanor added.

"Oh, Lord, it's why You came!" murmured Granny.

Granny was thinking of those who had been baptized into the Fermathe church. They and the hundreds more who were on her prayer list. Not that there were many saints among these still immature Christians, but that they were earnest about their need of the Christ they had pledged to grow like:

Soimeus, their pastor, was a good leader. He chose their own proverbs and folk tales to make his points. He could preach from the richness of his own experience with the Lord and his knowledge of the gospel message. He could quote passage after passage from the New Testament and apply it simply to the life they all shared there on the mountain slope. He would name this one or that for loyalty, for offerings given or withheld, for those acts becoming the Haitian Christian or shameful — such as attending a cockfight on a Sunday, one man taking another's wife, stealing his neighbor's machete, fighting, and many other sins of waywardness. So full was he of Christian zeal, his congregation stayed with him through praise and rebuke, favor and censure.

To develop a sense of moral values demands knowledge of his common culture. He laughs lustily at cheating and trickery. To cheat is clever. Except it is never smart to get caught. Only then does he repay, and verily under the ridicule of his friends. Wrongdoing is not penalized so much on a moral basis as on an economic one. An adulterous relation with another man's wife is settled with a cash adjustment. He took another man's property. To one whose conscience is clear until he is caught who has never known restraint in matters of sex it is not easy to understand the sin of a lustful eye. Sex has never had any moral implication for him. Relationships begin between youngsters. Normally young men and women live together without reproach. With maturity the male takes on family responsibilities but marriage is rare.

His concept of honesty runs a close parallel. He teaches his child a whole bag of tricks to haggle to beat the game if he can to go for the weak spots in another's armor. And he grows competent in sizing up his quarry. If he forfeits his machete, he is debased, but not for failure of character.

"But those who have espoused the Christian faith do honestly try hard to walk the straight and narrow," defended Wallace. "They fail much of the time because their background of evil betrays them. They actually can't span the spread between what comes naturally and Christ's teaching. If we had never had a twinge of conscience unless we were caught, had cleared the slate with an eye for an eye and a tooth for a tooth as the only way of keeping things even, it would be pretty hard to love a man who put a curse on your donkey, or stole your wife, or even broke your hoe.

It's hard for us to bless him who spitefully uses us. What if turning the other cheek brought intolerable ridicule and disgrace? You are a weakling and a coward. The taunts of the community can all but ostracize you. So you sin and return to the church to confess and pray. And the worst wife beater, scoundrel, and transgressor of them all can pray with such fervent contrition a saint would weep. Of those who have accepted the comforting news that God loves them and Jesus delivers them from their bondage of fear, there are many who can rightly be called saints."

But whatever the Christian demands to live the separated life, the touchstone of all tests is the cockfight. Cockfighting is Haiti's national sport. How many Americans would disavow football in a call for Christian denial? The Haitian Christian puts off the cockfight when he puts on the newness of life. Furthermore, he knows his pastor will be making the rounds of the Sunday afternoon cockfights.

"How did we ever put up with this failing in Keniel? Although Wallace insisted on efficiency, to work diligently was the last thing Keniel was equipped by nature to do," began Granny. "When I was holding down everything alone and twenty two Texas guests were coming for lunch, Keniel may have affairs to attend to at the cock ring. He may return for dinner and he may not. But Soimeus sees to it that no convert returns to the old life and cockfighting. He finally succeeded in maturing Keniel, who is one of our best teachers now." Granny continued musing as she turned the pages of the little book, God Is No Stranger.

Haitian Saints

There was Catule's gap-toothed smile. Granny could hear him pray, "Lord, our skin is black, but our sins are blacker. You have delivered us from sin and made us clean."

There was Juleps, his face alight with an inner glow. He loved to sing and his vibrant bass carried melody in any group. He prayed straight to the heart of God: "Lord, may your missionaries feel younger each day to distribute your Word. Give them zeal and keep them young and unwrinkled in their souls." And Granny never doubted the effectual fervor of his praying.

There was Julie who came with her small son and two gourdes. "The cyclone took my other three children. This is the only one left and I want to put him with you in the Lord's service. This money is for two months of schooling. I'll try to bring it every month to keep him in school."

Arnold brought his children in their regular shirt and pants. The cost of uniforms was too much, but he had sold the pig to have enough to let the girls, all of them, come to school also.

And there was Janoi. Janoi, the witch doctor, lived a short distance from the mission. He always took money for his cures, but when he became ill he came to the dispensary, bringing an onion or a little plum tree—something to pay. This had gone on twenty five years. Then came that never to be forgotten day when Janoi turned in his sins, his fetishes, his all, and joined with the rest of the redeemed in singing, Jesus Paid It All. Then he asked the members to tear down his temple, take the fetishes and charms with which his father before him had practiced his closely guarded magic, and burn them. A moving spectacle indeed. But not so much as one morning later on when, led by the pastor, they all went singing down to Granny's pond. The curious swelled the crowd, filling her entire sloping yard, and onlookers swayed with believers in rapt unison. The sun had just raised itself above the tops of the avocado trees, its long slanting rays fingers of benediction. When the pastor asked the old man for his confession he said fervently, "Oh, yes, I believe. The Lord let me live to bring others." (Before a new Christian can be accepted for membership he must prove his sincerity in his new faith by witnessing to others.) Who could see the light and peace in his old wrinkled face as he was carried under the pond waters and doubt the cleansing power of that hour?

Change

*Another wind, a wind
of hope and discovery,
is blowing across the
land. Who can say it will
not bring revolution?
Indeed, thirtyeight percent
of school age children in class is
revolutionary.*

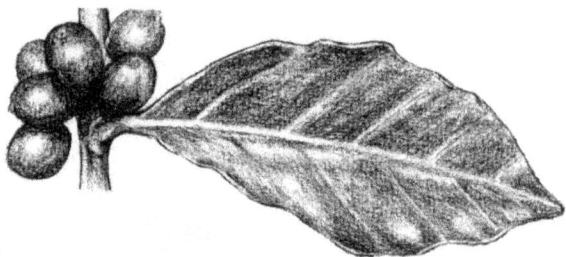

It was Sunday afternoon, and Eleanor had managed a little time apart with Granny and me. Dieula brought a pot and cups. As Eleanor poured the rich brew, she commented, "When the berries are picked ripe, roasted, ground, and prepared the same day, the result is superb coffee. Haitian coffee is excellent wherever it is served." She turned toward Granny's garden. "Granny's shrubs have been bearing for twenty five years. The coffee shrub grows from seven hundred to seven thousand feet up and once almost covered whole mountainsides from which the French colonials harvested millions of pounds annually. Today the product is lost for want of hands to gather it (slave stigma)."

Eleanor explained by turning back the pages of history.

Haiti's history is unique. When Columbus dropped anchor in the wide harbor off Cap Haïtien on Christmas Eve, 1492, he described the land as "all that man could desire." The Santa Maria broke up on a reef that night and Columbus left the ship's crew as a colony. These Spaniards undertook to enslave the friendly Arawak Indians who inhabited the island and many perished, but so had the colony when Columbus returned in 1498. The Spaniards spent fifty years attempting to establish a slave plantation system, but the Arawaks were so decimated by overwork, disease, suicide and persecution, their holders began stepping up importation of slaves from Africa. Anyway, the Spanish preferred pursuing gold in Mexico and Peru while using Haiti as an advantageous island base. Their conquistador successes soon lured the British buccaneers to raiding their treasure fleets. In fact, if tropical fever had not been Spain's ally the British would have wrested the Caribbean from Spanish control. The British did take over parts of Haiti. Later a British consul wrote: "In all the world there is not a country more suited to agriculture than Haiti; not one where the returns for labor are more magnificent; a rich, well-watered soil, where the growth of plants almost daily may be measured."

The French were next to claim the island. During French colonial days the chief product was sugar. In 1789 54,000,000 pounds of white sugar, 107,000,000 pounds of brown sugar, 71,000,000 pounds of coffee, went through the custom house, with 15,000,000 pounds reputed smuggled. The plantations provided cacao and bananas not only for French but many other European tables, literally requiring fleets to transport their superabundance. French historians never wearied of recounting the trade, the filled warehouses, the splendid estates and hillsides dotted with fine houses, the white population rich, refined, enjoying life as only a luxurious colonial society can enjoy it; the only dark spot, the mass of discontented black slavery. Ask these historians how was it the Spaniards established a system of slavery less cruel than the French. Anyway, the story holds that the Frenchman worked his Negroes inhumanely, then to quell discontent, punished them barbarously until on the eve of 1800 after one hundred years of slavery, these African descendants used the Voodoo drum to carry throughout the mountains the secret message signaling revolt. A noteworthy portion of these revolutionaries were mulatto freedmen offspring of white planters and slave mothers, who had sought political rights of the French. Some like Oge had been broken on the rack in Cap Haïtien for these demands. (An antique ink pot from his grandson-in-law is among the Turnbull bric-a-brac.)

In the blood and destruction that followed six hundred plantations and colonial homes were destroyed; only a few stone gateways still stand. Drunk on their carnage, the slaves were out of hand, when Toussaint, a former slave himself, took over leadership and drove out the white man entirely. The mulattos objected, but they too were quelled. Napoleon Bonaparte, embarrassed by the turn of events in France's most productive colony, sent his brother-in-law, LeClerc with 45,000 well trained troops to take the colony back. By deception LeClerc succeeded in capturing Toussaint and sent him to France to die a year later in a dungeon. But LeClerc lost both his life and his army to yellow fever. Toussaint's adjutants Henri Christophe and Dessalines accomplished what Toussaint set out to do. And, though they did not know it they thwarted Napoleon's intention of using the island as a springboard to establish a French empire in the new world, with Louisiana as its cornerstone. It was at this moment that President Jefferson sent James Monroe to the French court to negotiate the purchase of the port New Orleans and was offered all the French territory for $15, 000,000!

The Haitian patriot may have boasted that with his sugar cane knife he slaughtered and drove out the French, but he ignored two powerful allies, climate and yellow fever, which carried off a convincing number of his oppressors. The mosquito, carrier of malaria, another of yellow fever, fatal to Europeans but not to Africans, saved the land for them. Yellow fever is an endemic malady that exists only in countries which are warm the year around, where the native population is protected in childhood by a light form that gives immunity for life. Not so the foreigner. In 1800 the pick of Napoleon's troops landed in Haiti and in less than a year, yellow fever had vanquished the entire army, leaving the rebellious Haitians in possession of their soil.

The story also holds that many of these slaves were descendants of the Gold Coast Koromantee tribesmen. Renowned in Africa for their superior physique and fanatically libertarian spirit, these natives were brought over in great numbers, tricked or captured and sold to slave traders by warring tribes. Their descendants had developed guerrilla skills that aided their cause. Dessalines, uneducated and violent, had a reputation for ferocity and cruelty, which explains why the first decade of Haitian independence was no less than a dictatorship. Former slaves now found their freedom more burdensome than ever. After two years Dessalines was slain by his officers for his abuses. The entire 175-year history since then has been one contest after another for rule of the republic.

In 1805, the country was divided. General Pétion seized the south; Christophe the north. General Pétion, a cultured Creole educated in France, tolerant and democratic, gave away the land to the people. The policy inaugurated the self-sufficient, nonpolitical peasantry, which, although over regimented at that time, was able to overthrow Christophe a couple of decades later and reunite the island in poverty-stricken freedom. Meanwhile, Christophe, ruthless, hardworking, ambitious, prospered in the north and created a nobility. He read French papers, imitated Napoleon, introduced titles and an elegant court life that actually rivaled any in Europe. He built gigantic walls round half a dozen fortresses and stone coastal towers from which both sides of the ocean could be seen. He began building his palace at Milot and the awesome Citadelle above it.

Christophe had given the great estates to his courtiers. Production had decreased when the slaves left. Sugar was no longer exported, and its manufacture declined until it disappeared from the customhouse lists. That sugar making had been steeped in prejudice (only slaves worked in the fields) accounted for its decline. Cane is grown for making tafia, or white rum, and for molasses, which is used instead of sugar. Today there are only three sugar mills. Freeborn, the Haitian won't swap his shabby existence for any promise of mush and beans or any material thing to which he might become a slave; yet he knows that his property would not be respected during a revolution.

At first, the ex-slave was given a plot of ground and told that a canal would someday provide water. He reverted to the slash and burn farming of his African ancestors, who could migrate from place to place, leaving charred and spent land behind them. Only a hurricane could have been more destructive of his land than the years of struggle since his freedom. Although unable to migrate, the Haitian's corn and millet needed little care; he had coffee and fruits and wild game, even up on the high mountains. So he wantonly cut the trees for charcoal to cook his mush and to sell in Port-au-Prince. His shelter was simple, as it had always been, a thatched roof, the furnishings a millstone and a flat grinding table, some gourd water pots, and if he was well off, a canari (water jar). His clothing was a breechcloth in summer and a Lindsey shirt and pants in the cooler months. There was time for talk and laughter, a little weaving, fashioning a machete, and for long rituals of religion. Even in a drought year when dry winds swirled the ashes in his dooryard and burned his corn on the young stalk, there was something to find for food. In the marshes were wild geese and ducks in the thickets, wild pigeons and nuts. Decade after decade he continued to dance and sing, court, play simple games, appease the spirits, live and die this generation about the same as the one before. But each abuse of nature's bounty contrived more want.

Both Eleanor and Granny offered to sum up the Haitian's plight:

The rural Haitian is uneducated. There is little public education. The Haitian people object to direct taxation so the government must rely on import and export duties; hence the income of the republic depends chiefly on the custom-house.

"That's why we can't welcome any kind of parcel. Try to understand how involved it becomes to wait most of the day at douane (customs) to have the package opened, its contents named and valued; go to the bank and wait to buy tax stamps, return to customs again and have the stamps verified; wait for an extremely pedantic Haitian clerk to look up your items in several places in his book, make entries in four places in two colors of ink, then multiple copies; then consult his superiors and get two or three of their signatures, then finish by having you sign in several places, and you finally claim the parcel which has cost you twice its original cost in the States, and by now may have been pilfered."

But reform and change are in the mill from the bottom. The Communists have shunned Haiti because there is no wage-supported laboring class no landed gentry and no land to divide. The Haitian farmer has been written off as a hopeless dropout from the rest of the world.

With his back to the denuded mountain steeps with no place to go for escape his primitive mind is about to accept change from within.

When nineteen year old Jean Claude Duvalier assumed his father's title President-à-Vie he proposed to carry through his father's five stage plan: 1) social reform, 2) economic revolution, 3) education, 4) industrial progress, and 5) cultural revolution. His first step was to relax the police atmosphere by removing from public his father's Tonton Macoutes.

To the rural person comprising ninety five percent of the population, evil exists in the palace, the tax collector, the informers and the executioners, and those who become rich on the periphery. However those who once exploited the masses in shops and legal wiles, and who remain aloof in their French culture are enjoying fewer of these inherited advantages. The president, disturbed by the dried-up tourist traffic, offered duty-free wares to the tourist shopper. This exemption was rescinded when the store owners were found to be taking home most of the duty-free English porcelains, French perfumes, Danish silver, Italian carvings, Japanese radios and cameras, British tweeds, Swiss watches, and American TV sets. These families of wealth send their children to France to be educated, and lately to the United States. The new generation educated are forsaking the old culture and traditions, their daughters often preferring to marry foreigners and not return to the island of their birth, their sons choosing to seek the challenges of the space age in other lands, instead of the challenge of political problem solving in Haiti.

Both the weakness and the strength of Haiti are in these rural people, who are convinced that evil comes from the capital. Now that they are seeing education in a new and different light, it may be that they will not be so slow to pick up the reins of government when their literacy rate is reversed.

Change is about to promote change, change from within.

It must be admitted that the Haitian values his own culture, as does the European or American, and he weighs what he finds. His old way will have both functional and symbolic importance to him, which one inviting him to change does not ignore. That he can and will change is history. How could the culture of the black have undergone more far-reaching change than what has been achieved in the States during slavery and afterward?

Granny seemed to view a not too distant future. "When we came to Haiti ninety eight percent of the people could not read or write their name. In the beginning, long before we even had a convert, when we would gather a group for a service, we announced there would be school the next morning, and we began to teach them. 'You don't want your children to grow up without schooling, do you? We'll expect to see them tomorrow at the mission school to hear God's word and to learn to read and write.' Then I would walk these mountain trails three days a week to persuade parents to let their children come. I would sew up a little garment for each child who came. First, only two or three, then gradually there were forty, despite the discouraging attitude of parents and friends. As time went on and the work grew, there were two hundred children enrolled at the mission. One hundred thirty five outreach churches in time attracted 15,000 children to mission schools—the only education available in the mountains. As our Christians learned, they would go to a neighboring area, win converts, start a church, and begin a literacy class.

"As more and more learned to read, a whole new era was born in rural Haiti. Parents who had argued, 'Why should my child be bothered with city ways?' now said, 'If Jacques' child can learn to read, so can mine.' Where only two decades ago the written word was virtually unknown, now education is vigorously pursued. Streams of children in school uniforms daily line the roads."

Granny's Each One-Teach-One

"Indeed!" added Eleanor, "Respect for learning has grown so much, parents beg to do any menial job to get the few cents to keep their children in school. The opportunity and responsibility settled upon the mission churches. In every isolated area, Christians came together to work out ways to start a one teach one four level school. That was Granny's idea, and her method was to pay each child who had learned to read when he taught another."

Granny chuckled. "Since only twenty out of a hundred school age children were in our mission schools, the other eighty began showing increasing eagerness to learn to read and write. I felt sorry and knew that the Lord would help me do something for them. So I began offering our children who had gone to school ten cents per child per month for each child they taught the three R's they had learned. Of course, our children began using the choruses and hymns and Bible verses they had learned in Sunday school. They were even teaching the little learners to pray. Soon there were fifteen of these schools going, with from twenty to a hundred children in each school. I gave a first grade reader and piece of chalk to each group, each day. The lesson would be written on a makeshift blackboard for all to see. A sharpened stick on the path or a beaten smooth area under a brush cover would serve for practice sessions."

No money for this project was available through the mission budget, so Granny had to rely on faith and gifts from friends to finance this burgeoning enterprise.

"Never less than $70.00 a month, and my commitment increases as the project spreads," admitted Granny, gravely. "Swamped. The Lord and I are in it together," she concluded.

She had been fed by the ravens so long, she could see only the Lord's blessing. Then, reminding herself that tomorrow would be

Monday and she must go teach the teachers the Sunday school lesson for next Sunday, she rose to go. Why on Monday morning? "So they can live it all the week," she insisted!

Cotton grows perennially in Haiti. Women use the dropped spindle method to spin fiber.

Grannyese

Granny never makes one think she's pious or self-righteous.
She has a bubbling sense of humor and laughs gustily at her own jokes.

In those early days, because they were so ragged, so unwashed, so illiterate, Granny admits that she would cry. "Thirty years ago this was wild, remote country, no road, no resort or summer homes of those from the city up this way, as now. We had few visitors from the outside. The peoples' needs so painfully outweighed our deeds, I would cry. I knew it wasn't good, so I used to call the signal and make myself laugh anyway, a grim humor though it was. When a mother would bring her young one for worm medicine, and I would tell her to hold his nose and open his mouth, she would say to the child, 'It's sweet syrup!' I'd say, 'No, it's not. It smells and tastes bad, but you want to get well'... The mama would come again with, 'It's sweet syrup', and I'd say, 'No,, then think, 'How ludicrous is our useless contention!' "

Sugar and grain bags, boldly printed in bright colors, were prized by the rural people, who made them into dresses for the women and sleeveless shirts for the men. Washing was often postponed so the red and blue printing would not fade out. One day a man came to Granny's class with "Low in fiber, high in protein" across the front of his shirt. Later a woman's skirt proclaimed "100 pounds net." Both advertised turkey feed.

The boys in her English class were having trouble with prepositions. One asked, "Do the women in the U.S. carry anything in their heads?" "Some do," admitted Granny. (Women carry everything on their heads in Haiti.)

Most of Granny's friends know by now that they can't give her something

for herself. She will give it away. One of the Port-au-Prince doctors who came up to the mission hospital for clinic days, was getting married. Granny brought a new sheet and two pillowcases by the office, asking that it be wrapped and sent down before Dr. Etienne's wedding. Gladys found still tucked in a fold: "This is a little gift for you, Granny, from the Missionary Cupboard. May the Lord keep you in His arms always. First Baptist Church, St. Cloud, Minn."

Familiar to every convert who came to Granny's learners' class is Granny teaching with her Bible in hand.

One day the mission will have telephone service from the city. Already the cable is being laid above Petionville, on its way to the President's summer home a few miles below the mission. But if the jeep had not caught fire and claimed all of David's vacation visit rebuilding it, he might have worked on an intercom system for the compound. Next vacation, he promises to reactivate the battery of old military phones presently adorning Eleanor's kitchen wall. Granny might find a telephone more convenient than a courier. Although she usually can find a runner, sometimes she has to stop what she's doing and go herself. Her messages to Wallace and Eleanor and any of the other individuals around the busy compound are penciled notes on the back of any old envelope, wrapper, or scrap paper. These communiqués save time for her own busy schedule, for, likely as not, she spares herself waiting around awhile, especially if she wants to see someone at the Turnbull ménage. Waiting around is not for Granny. "There's too much to do. I won't spend what time I have left waiting around." Her hurriedly penned notes may imply urgency or necessity, or may hint of dilemma or impasse.

To have been able to telephone would have saved much of the day when she went with Antoine to town in the jeep to pick up some goods at the freight depot, and she found herself stalled in an unpreventable situation. Although Eleanor knew that she could take a jeep ride with the hardiest commuter, she felt a little uneasiness when the trip had taken too long. In time, a runner arrived with a note written on some bagging. Stranded several miles down the mountain, Granny pled: "Eleanor, here we are by Moise's house with an immovable jeep loaded to the bodyguards. Not a drop of oil does it have. All the rubber plugs are burned out. Would you ask the Help women to let you have their car to come for us? The jeep cannot be used. Granny."

Verily, waiting idly is more intolerable to Granny than a flogging. One Tuesday, ready to teach in the Bible Institute, she went to class at 8:15 a.m. No one was there. When she came to the office and learned that her class didn't meet until 11:00 a.m. on Tuesday and Thursdays, she said, "I'll have time to shred the cabbage for several jars of sauerkraut before eleven. When we take Jesus at His word to go, make disciples, and teach them, He meant everything we know, even how to make sauerkraut."

Another time, "Eleanor, what can I do for supper? I have a half hour before class." Eleanor suggested dessert. Thirty minutes later Granny sent over a banana pudding, steaming from the oven.

Granny had dressed some chickens and wanted to singe away the pin feathers. Out of old paper, she came by the office and asked Joyce, "May I have your wastebasket? I need some scrap paper."

Another time she sent a note up to Joyce to ask for a name and address, but she must have felt pretty helpless. "Send me the name of the board member in Minneapolis who gave and installed the generator so we could have light when we have a blackout. I need his caponizing tools if I'm to teach Alouest how to de-sex the chickens. Please. Please. Granny."

Granny's image may be most familiarly cast with her sitting on the edge of a table, her Bible in hand, with thirty or more learners gathered around her memorizing 1 Thessalonians 5:21: *Prove all things, retaining only what is good and rejecting all that has a look of evil about it.*

Family and friends were enjoying breakfast in Eleanor's kitchen. The morning sun streamed across the grey and white tile, through a collection of blue and green bottles, to the table. Dieula had gone outside to help Jeta shell cashews on the kitchen steps. Eleanor had brought Zenas his black olives and started to suggest plans for the day when Granny reached the door. She was clutching some marigold plants along with a pan of fresh meat while removing her mud-soiled shoes at the door. Would she join the group for coffee? No, after a couple of hours' work in the garden she had made breakfast at home. Could Dieula take the marigolds up to the roadside stand? She needed to be at the playground where already there was a loud Saturday morning jubilee. (All the children from good homes down the mountain were gathering for the weekly Bible story hour. The attractive designer from New York who had taken the spacious new Mediterranean villa above Petionville had brought her two youngsters; so had the writer and his wife brought their two. There were the children of the engineer and one of the developers of the island of Tortuga, the daughter of the contractor building the new resort hotel, the children of the couple working with the Food for Work program, and children of older residents. Granny's stories were dear to all of them, as were the good times afterward on the volleyball court.)

Granny's home has been a rest stop and purlieu for other missionaries. They come up for a respite from overwork and isolation, the heat of the lowlands, and even TB.

Granny remembers when she was a candidate for appointment to Africa and a mission board member had asked, "Can you get along with other Christians?" "Oh, yes," she had replied, and thought, what a silly question. Now she says, after being on the mission field, it was the most important question of all. "You are on Satan's territory when on the mission field, and Satan is a past master at causing discord. Discord hinders the gospel message more than all the excesses." Long since having learned to quell a hint of conflict, with determined grace, Granny has become the perfect antidote for washing away on the field biliousness.

Seeking privacy in Haiti is wasted effort. You seek in vain. And you soon relax when you discover that the rural people are unimpressed by the unclad human figure.

Granny never makes one think she's pious or self-righteous. She has a bubbling sense of humor and laughs gustily at her own jokes, such as: In those days when mirrors weren't in general use, a woman had been observing her husband taken something from his pocket, study it with satisfaction, then put it back in his pocket. "Well," she concluded, "he has the portrait of another woman." Fired with jealousy, she arose in the night after her husband was asleep, searched his pockets and found the object she sought. Looking at it, she decided, "Well, if that is what attracts him so much, I have no reason to worry."

Hurt when she is scolded for climbing on a ladder or tabletop, Granny goes in her garden to work with her flowers, murmuring, "You are there where I put you, you're not rude, and you don't talk back!"

When the family urges her to go along to the city or on a day long trip, she might decline. "No. Associate with young people to stay young; try to keep up with them and you get old."

So often do friends and visiting groups ask to take her picture, she has been heard to remark, "The hardest part of missionary life is the picture taking."

Granny grows little chickens, thirty in a coop. When those at the mission stop by her house, she is sure to say, "Before you get started, I want you to see my chickens."

She stays for supper at the Turnbulls only now and then. It takes too long. "Why eat yogurt when you get the same nutrition drinking a glass of buttermilk? No, I can't stay for supper. The boys are waiting to have English class."

When house guests and the family linger and chat over coffee at the breakfast table, Granny might drop in, mud on her shoes from the garden. Her smile with lifted eyebrows plainly says, "It's seven thirty. Not at work yet!"

Granny's prayers betray her most. She talks with the Lord like a gardener making up his rows. She names them one by one, asking grace for Simon who must get his hernia repaired, Altagrace who is left with five little girls, Tiya who is doing all he can but it's not enough to keep body and soul together for his little family, Muna who is trying so hard to learn to read God's Word, Maricia who wants to follow the Lord but her backsliding is getting to be chronic, then those at the mission, those back in the States. She will come with a new list next time. However, she may say often, "Lord, your banner over us is love!" Or at the table, "Lord, we thank you for this food. Thank you for Jesus, the Bread of Life, and help us to feed our souls on Him!"

———

Some who visit the island and see a Voodoo ceremony return home to shock home folk with this horror mysticism. To Granny it's just plain Satan. Simple as that.

Frugality has become a way of life for Granny. She never discards string, a board, a piece of iron, or even a rag. Jars and containers for her pickles and preserves and sauerkraut are greater gifts than a lovely new sweater. When she returns to Haiti, her baggage bulges with seeds and bulbs and communion cups. And school supplies, or even a piano, and other much needed goods, the largess of friends will follow by freight.

Granny's frugality is legendary. She needed a few things for relish she would make one day. To one of the summer students going down to the city she sent a note: "Scott, please see if you can find three red sweet peppers at the Iron Market, maybe for one or two cents each. Try for one cent even if not too fresh. Thanks. Granny."

———

Everybody agrees that Granny can make a dollar go farther than most people can make ten dollars go. The newest building for the mission will be Sunday school rooms. On an old envelope she challenges Eleanor: "Eleanor, if you will donate the syrup, I'll donate all else, and every bottle of syrup will give us $4.00 for the

Sunday School Building. I'll also donate $50.00 that is on hand that the pickles and preserves and peanut brittle made, so if you have ten bottles of syrup, we'll have $90.00 for our new building. It counts up. Granny."

So sure was Granny that her pickles and such would sell at the new Mountain Maid Tearoom, she sent a note up to Joyce: "Please make a sign advertising these as delicacies:

Dill pickles, each 5¢
Relish, jar 75¢
Sweet pickles jar $1.00
Pickled Onions jar 80¢
Strawberry Jam, $1.50
Raspberry Jelly, large $1.50 "

Hardly the epicure who is ready to trade recipes or titillate over a taste treat with Granny, Wallace knows he understates her culinary wizardry when he is heard to say, "She always sets a good table." A year or so before, when somebody had mentioned that horseradish, along with coriander, nettle, horehound and lettuce, was one of the five bitter herbs of the Passover, Granny had insisted that horseradish is seldom bitter until it's three months old, and Wallace had confessed, now forgotten, a yen for some of this nippy herb. Granny, on her next trip to the States, did not forget.

At length the time came when Wallace learned for sure where he dwelt in Granny's affections. It was the first day of October. Schools would be opening all over the island. Church leaders and all looked to Pastor Turnbull for counsel and aid in coping with the problems of an unprecedented turnout of children eager to begin the new school year—teachers to hire and pay, canteens to keep going, meager supplies to make do, and scores of shortages. Wallace, weary from a hard two week jeep and horseback tour of eighteen outposts and all their uncombed problems, reached home at dusk. Greeting and answering everybody's questions at once, he settled in his place at the table. Thankful that supper featured meat, he noted a small jar with a note at his plate.

Wallace opened the note. "Wallace, here is your horseradish. Any motherinlaw who would bring the plant from the States, grow it, dig the root, and grate it, must love her son-in-law. Oh, the tears I've shed over this horseradish! It may bring tears to your eyes, for it's undiluted, 100% pure. And loads of love come with it. Granny."

Celebrities

Dodo took her place late at the breakfast table. "Five ships drop anchor in the bay today," she announced calmly.

"Oh, yes, Albert Mangones sent word for us to drop by after the opening." Others at the table knew that Eleanor indicated the Habitation LeClerc, Haiti's newest and perhaps the most chic hotel in the Caribbean.

Back in 1961, Katherine Dunham, professional dancer, singer and anthropologist, purchased, refurbished, and opened a place on the 260 yea rold estate that was once Pauline LeClerc's palace. It is almost a part of Port-au-Prince to the south. Katherine and her Bohemian crowd—artists, dancers, actors—used it as a gathering place until she persuaded Laurence Peabody and Ari Onassis to restore the palace. Pauline was Napoleon Bonaparte's sister, who came to Haiti as a seventeen year old bride of Napoleon's governor general, Charles LeClerc.

The original fourteen acres of the park, a jungle of majestic breadfruit, mango and bamboo trees, surround the new Habitation, which incorporates the restored swimming pool, stone sculptures, courtyard fountain, and some of the original walls. Three handsome crystal chandeliers grace the arcaded marble gallery entrance. Around the palace are three or four guest houses, each with its swimming pool, cobblestone walks, and marble statuary set amid lush tropical plantings.

The architect was Albert Mangones, Cornell graduate and husband of French artist Adelaide Mangones. He designed the outlet shop for the mission and the new apartments.

"Look for some of the celebrities after the opening," said David.

"We're easier to find today than when Leonard Bernstein came," recalled Granny. "Back in 1954 Wallace was driving up the mountain in the jeep. He became a little annoyed by two Americans in shorts beeping behind him, and as soon as he could pull over, he let them pass. The driver called out asking if he knew a good place to eat. 'Sure. Our place. Follow me. Right close,' Wallace shouted back. When they got to the house they introduced themselves as Mr. and Mrs. Leonard Bernstein. That meant nothing to me then. They saw that they had come to a private home, so they asked if a hotel or restaurant was close by. No, Wallace insisted that since I was having Howard Seidner and his bride Rosalyn of Chicago and the Turnbulls for lunch, two more would be the merrier. Rosalyn suspected that they were sharing the company of famous people. At length she asked if Mr. Bernstein had spoken in her synagogue about six weeks ago. He had."

After the treat of hot dogs which a missionary friend had left, homemade bread and butter and hot tea, everybody went up the mountain to the resort Kenscoff, leaving Granny two or three hours in which to prepare dinner of roast beef, vegetables, rice and black mushrooms, and mango shortcake. That evening, at Granny's table laid with her best linen and china, Bernstein remarked, "I've had an opera festering in my mind for years, an opera on Voodoo..." (He later said it flopped)... Howard quipped, "It would have had a good chance to fester this afternoon. We must have seen the worst of Haiti. Eleanor lanced a lip festering with a chique flea. A TB patient lay hemorrhaging on the roadside. Another died of cancer of the hip..." He paused, then resumed with more pleasant adventures of the day.

When they left, Bernstein hugged and kissed Granny, with, "Granny, you are wonderful!" To which Granny has added many times in relating the story, "Take heart, girls, I waited sixty two years before being hugged by a famous man!"

A neighbor agronomist, Atherton Lee, once brought Henry Wallace over to the mission. A candidate for the Presidency, Wallace was convinced that the United States food giveaway policy should be replaced by medical and school programs or work relief programs. If food is given for work, he reasoned with Wallace agreeing, self-esteem is preserved and native workers in time will have roads and houses and education for their children.

The time Euell Gibbons brought his wife up to the mission he found the gardening at the compound impressive. Cattails, base of stem and roots, are edible, Haitians did not know, but fennel, purslane, lambsquarters, sourgrass and other wild greens are being ignored. He exulted over the watercress.

And Pétion Savain often found his way up to the mission. On one of his visits he left the painting that adorns Eleanor's living room wall. He died in 1973.

And Jack Bailhe, bon vivant special services adventurer of Basque, sent by the American government to Southeast Asia as a liaison with French colonial natives, came with cyclic welcome. No evening lacked willing ears for this raconteur.

And the Governor General of Jamaica for whom Granny put on extra turnips and boiled beef.

And how many times have Colonel Keyes and the chaplain flown over from Gitmo with a delightful couple, as yesterday, when the colonel unloaded some surplus paint, two cases of canned goods, and some oh-so-dear roofing. When Chaplain McDonald transferred from Gitmo to Corpus Christi, Texas, he booked Granny to speak in one of the Corpus Christi churches on her next deputation visit to the States.

The day the captain of the S.S. Seattle brought a Navy Handclasp shipment of school and medical supplies and tarried for lunch, was like rain breaking the drought.

And there was the visit in June 1973 of Liberia's President Tolbert with his first lady and two daughters. Tolbert had been vice president twenty years under Tubman and one of the daughters had married a Tubman son. Being a Baptist, President Tolbert had accepted the Turnbull invitation to visit the mission, after seeing them at

the palace reception for heads of state. Prior to their visit, David and Chris had done a professional taxidermy job with two beautiful flamingos which now graced the Turnbull foyer. (Wallace used to take his rifle when he visited churches in the coast al area where pink flamingos are plentiful. Until recently no game laws prevented his bagging a couple on one of these trips.) Mrs. Tolbert took such a liking to the flamingos, Eleanor insisted the foyer needed only one, which it now has.

Often a guest at the mission, Seldon Rodman, writer and collector of art, so drawn to the Haitian open-heartedness and natural appeal, he acquired a great love for the island.

And the Vinks, Vietnamese couple of noble descent who headed the United Nations contingent for the island, came as oft as any. Ruth Dayan, also with the United Nations when she first visited Haiti, was attracted to the native handicraft skills, and spent much time at the mission noting their techniques and later collecting rarer carvings and weavings.

"Granny is wonderful," declares international socialite Mrs. Horace Ashton who comes up for flowers and plants. While lingering over tea she might, in her lilting way, recall a time at Ascot, Newbury or Churchill Downs, or the week she attended the wedding of Grace Kelly and Prince Rainier.

Dr. Comer, Colorado University anthropologist, made a number of palmy visits to the mission. He found the mission children an optimum cold frame for studies on sociologic changes occurring in emerging primitive peoples.

Often Harvard teams, sent to Haiti from the Department of Public Health, became manna to the mission's better family hygiene effort, and gilded many an evening with conversation that bred lasting friendships.

Not every day brings a celebrity. There was the day the pair of hippies drifted in from New York and stayed so long the whole compound sighed with relief when they departed. Their hair, long with the latest admired untidiness, scandalized Granny as much as the girl's brief minis and see-through blouses. Another time

Granny came home to find eleven hippies surrounding her open refrigerator, helping themselves.

There are always the displaced students of mixed nationality. The immature blond from Oregon, too young to sort the rigors of the mission field in equatorial Africa; the stream of those who had bad trips and near disasters with drugs; the ever-present curious, the freeloaders, and always those who came uninvited, perhaps to stay weeks. Could they have found this home atmosphere the kindliest they had ever known, or the first understanding warmth in their lives? Nobody is turned away. But usually guests do some kind of work if they stay awhile. A culinary talent may very well train Dieula and Jetée in the fine art of making cheese-onion pie, black bean cassoulet, or chocolate rum roll. A man with talent may instruct some of the Haitian boys in woodcarving or in animal husbandry.

And there was the UP reporter Betty Johnson whose idea of adventure never included anything so raw as Haiti after the 1965 landslide, but who had to take some pictures back with her, so she made off with Wallace's, which he had sent out by runner to Granny to be developed.

With work more the norm than usual on the eve of the Turnbulls, departure for the States for Sandy's and Mary's wedding in August, nobody was expecting, or was vestmented to receive Haiti's head of state. Yet the drop-in visit of smiling young President Jean Claude Duvalier sent the whole compound into a flurry of welcome and accommodation. A runner went for Wallace and Eleanor and Granny. And although none could match the dash of the entourage of colonels and cavalier retainers who crowded the tearoom that afternoon, the warm atmosphere of exchange that prevailed braced the young president's promise to come again.

And come again he did by proxy, on Granny's ninetieth birthday, when she herself was a celebrity. Everybody at the mission had pulled out all the stops, and an unprecedented assemblage swelled the throng on that happy occasion. Granny's only surviving sister, Granny's son, and scores of Stateside friends came to brighten the day. Hundreds of others, including President and Mrs. Carter, sent messages or remembrances.

A special service at the Fermathe church recalled how things were when Granny's ministry began with them over three decades before. Most had shared Granny's Bible and English classes, which always began with Thy Word Have I Hid in My Heart. These words, meaningful to all, a young mother sang in dedication of the day. This tribute meant as much to Granny as any of the happenings of the day.

At the reception which followed, everybody mixed and mingled and sampled the birthday cake. Special yellow rose-encrusted creation of a Port-au-Prince baker friend, the cake's surprise adornment was a set of toy garden tools.

Later in the day, the compound still milling with the gay throng, Eleanor missed Granny. Had the excitement been too much for her? Eleanor slipped away from the crowd and ran down to Granny's house. There was Granny, checking on her newest brood of baby chicks, by now noisily clamoring for their overdue supper.

Haitiana

Hearing children called by such names as Merci Dieu (Thank God), Predernier (Almost Last), C'est Tout (That's All), Beni Soit (Blest Be), Dieu Donne (God Gave) grows provocative.

Often the baby is called the first word that escapes the mother's lips when the baby is born, and thereafter is a charm protecting the child.

If Dieu Donne had been less comely, the euphony of her name might be lost on her. But graceful as a doe, bright-eyed and smiling, she reflects the natural gaiety of her people.

Jesula (Jesus There), flip and pert, learns quickly, seldom needs to be told twice. Clever and willing is not all. Unhappily, she bears watching.

Bene Soit is patient and enduring, by virtue of a durable African ancestry.

Nazila is not half as hard on the ears as on the sensitivity when one learns that a city sophisticate once suggested the name in mischief (donkey). But Nazila, very black, her body straight as a palm trunk, moves with a lioness' stride. She may prance in savage triumph over Mona's backwardness in the kitchen.

Telephone abides in Anse Rouge, Sterile not far down the mountain. There are many Dieulas (God There) and Jesulas (Jesus There).

Choose your camion for blessing and benediction. Obviously christened for charmed life, these incredibly overloaded, gaily colored, careening, cavorting buses court the guardianship their names imply: Our Shield and Strength, Be My Guide, Guardian Angel, Manor of Angels, Gospel According to John, St. Joseph, Rock of My Refuge. If a Maude or In Spite of All covets protection and passengers, they undoubtedly were saints confused. And since Port-au-Prince is a place where the Word of God runs to and fro in free course, take care lest it run you down!

Somebody important dies. There are happenings in the palace and in the marketplace. Yet the villagers without modern means of communication knows of today's goings-on. How? Teledyol! (Telemouth) Word of mouth sends messages over the country in hours. People dare not use written messages, telephone, or telegraph. Palace scuttlebutt reaches to the remotest areas in hours.

If two foreigners have a dispute, do nothing.
If a foreigner and a Haitian have a dispute, favor the Haitian.
If two Haitians have a dispute, favor the one higher in government.

The mission was getting electricity. Poles were being dragged and spaced for the lines. Two mountain boys who had never been away from their isolation, looking down across the valley at the vehicles, beeping, cried: "Look! Big pigs climb up the mountain!"

During the hurricane rehabilitation, cheese was issued in wedges cut from round hoops. Mona brought hers back. "It does not lather," she complained.

⸎

A young man wanted to marry Rezie who worked in the kitchen at the mission. He wanted to set the time and marry her in March. The Turnbulls explained that they would be away in March and suggested that the wedding date be set for the last Saturday in February. "No. Forget the whole matter."

⸎

To relieve a woman in pains of childbirth: Make a tea of dirt from all four corners of the house, leaves of verbena (sedative), elmwood, write the woman's name on paper, burn it and mix the ashes in the tea. Go to the rear of the house, face the east, and call her three times. She must answer to the third, then give her the mixture. She will be relieved. If it's a boy, name him Emmanuel.

⸎

How to care for a fighting cock:: Put a piece of ox tongue, seven verbena leaves, a handful of earth, verbena root, a few ginger roots and some pimiento. Grind up and put in alcohol with a little gunpowder and incense and rub into the cock's body.

⸎

The witch doctor's bag (alfor) might contain lizard, frog, bat, chicken, and snake bones, cloves of garlic, wax candles, nails, pins, thread, dove hearts, mole skins, small mirrors, sulphur, salt, alum, and poisonous herbs to make charms (ouangas).

⸎

Until very recently every family had a slave. After the hurricanes, forty cents for a child was a bargain, for birth papers went with the child and all right to the child was yielded irrevocably. If asked, "How can you add another to the family?" the reply was typically Haitian, "If one eats, all will eat. If none eats, all fast."

⸎

Marie chased her chicken into Pestil's "tied" garden. Her child fell ill and the neighbors declared the child would die of the curse. A follower of the New Way, she nonetheless went to the witch doctor to remove the curse. The church deacons say she doubted.

※

Mother to children carrying gourds of water up the trail: "Courage, small ones. Come up so I can take the water for you."

※

Andre's grandfather was a general in the Haitian army. He was out on the trail one night alone. A black man crossed his path and said, "Whatever crosses your path farther up the trail, put it around your neck." A snake crossed his path. He grabbed it and put it around his neck and it became a gold chain. On that date each year thereafter, he would retire to his room alone for a time, during which he would take off his chain, thread it down a bottle of champagne and watch his patron saint drink it.

※

The child who falls down and breaks the gourd bringing up water is roundly scolded if not punished when he returns to the caille. Bottles and tin cans make prized possessions. A milk can becomes a lamp to light at dusk, a cooking or watering pot. Otherwise, clay jars which have been baked in a kiln after finishing with rubbing by the women, become the water "canaris" in which they cool and store drinking water.

※

Marillia had lost her baby. She came to work with a red rag tied around her big toe so her milk couldn't go to her head.

Marie's child had died and she tied a red string around the two siblings, arms so "the little one can't come back to play with them."

※

Emile came to work tired, his long face twitching. He declared that he had seen the albino sorceress. She visits you in the night and afflicts you with worms. Here, as in other parts of the world, the albino is an accursed being. Outcast of the community, this

184

unfortunate is doomed to a life of darkness and superstitious rejection by even family and neighbors.

While luxury hotels, swank boutiques and elegant restaurants compete for the tourist's wallet, the sun-dappled streets along the waterfront of Port-au-Prince offer special allurement as well as a unique portrait of Haitian philosophy and life in the primitive oils that line the streets.

With a self-taught technique that seems three-dimensional, Haiti's primitive artists delineate village life, flowers, waterfalls, mountain roads, cock fighting, open-air markets, and the sea, with startling clarity. Their oils are brilliant, even violently so. The murals of Toussaint Auguste, Prefete Dufaut, Philome Pierre, Obin, Benoit, and Bazile gained international acclaim when they were given a free hand with the interior of the Episcopal Trinity Cathedral. Other famous artists are Hippolite, Bigaud, Antonio, Josèf, Adam Leontus, Gesner Abelard, and Domond.

Sculptors, also mostly self-taught, carve stunning primitive figures of mahogany.

Haitian Heartstrings

Introducing a visiting preacher to the Fermathe flock, the pastor prayed: "Lord, we know that with you nothing is difficult. We know that once you spoke your message through a donkey. Today we ask that you do the same thing as we turn the service over to our visiting brother."

Word had come that a new hurricane Beulah was threatening. A new convert prayed in church: "Lord, we hear that your hurricane is coming, but we ask you now to reach out, take it, wad it in a ball, and pitch it far out to sea." (The prayer was answered; the hurricane went out to sea.)

There is a Creole proverb that weeds have ears because someone is hiding in them. Prayed one, "Oh, Lord, we know you have big, big ears to hear us."

"Lord, the way we complain and cry with tears falling like rain, people will say our mothers bore us during a storm."

"Lord, you told us to go to the ant. He never went to school, he has no degree, and his brain is too small to see, but he's a master workman. I have never been to school, I can't calculate, and I don't have much brain either. But Lord, make me a master workman in your kingdom, and let others come and learn and say, 'That's God in him'."

"Lord, we're like a frog puffed with air and getting over-big when someone criticizes us. Pierce us and let the air out."

"In every house Problem has a reserved chair where he sits. In every church Problem has a reserved chair where he sits. Only Love can persuade Problem to give up his seat."

"Look at the reed that sways and bends under the weight of the bird that lights on it, yet it always holds him. Be sure that God knows our frailty and weighs the burden he places on us."

"Father, we are all hungry baby birds this morning. Our heart-mouths are gaping wide for you to fill us."

"Lord, our skin is black, but our sins are blacker; but you have delivered us from Satan and made us white."

"Father, we ask that you give wings to your Word that is preached—not the wings of an airplane that passes far over our heads, but the wings of a bird which lights and rests in the trees. Let your Word rest with us."

"Now, Lord, we want you to come and stand beside us. Take your hand and put one finger in this ear (right). But, Lord, don't take your hand and put a finger in the other ear (points left), because we want what the preacher says to go in this ear (points) but not out this ear (points to other ear)."

"Lord, as husks cooked in the mush sets off coughing, so does trash in our Christian lives set off the unsaved. Lord, wash us and pour off the husks, and cook us into good mush."

⸺⸺

"Lord, without you we are without a brace. A roof without a brace will fall in."

⸺⸺

"Like the woman, Lord, who was refused oil because her bottle was dirty, we stand before you ashamed and ask that you clean us up before you put your oil in."

⸺⸺

"The Voodoo drums beating is like rats gnawing. Where the sickness is, we must take the medicine."

⸺⸺

"When a Christian pulls up his stake and sets it over, he's setting his boundary on someone else's land (the world evil)."

⸺⸺

"Spit into the air and spittle falls in your face."

⸺⸺

"Lord, there's a big devil called Discouragement. We ask you to send him away, because he is bothering us."

⸺⸺

"Lord, we lack clothes to wear to church, we lack food at home, and we lack two cents in our pocket, but we don't lack the grace of Jesus. With that grace we are rich." (Prayer after drought.)

⸺⸺

"Lord, help us to leave our mouth at home, and come with our heart, head, ears, and heed to you, our boss."

⸺⸺

"Father, when the baby cries, the mother gives the breast. Let the Holy Spirit be our breast to console and nourish us."

Haitian Proverbs

The empty sack cannot stand.

Behind the mountains are more mountains.

Never buy a cat in a feed bag.

A scalded cat is afraid even of cold water.

It takes much water to wash a mud hut.

Before you put a snake to school, you have to teach him to sit on a bench.

A wooden door doesn't fight with an iron door.

An earthen jug doesn't battle with an iron jug

Farmers don't stay long in town.

You can't put both feet in one shoe.

A dog has four paws, but he can go only one way.

Genius is akin to madness.

John seeks, John finds, John is encumbered.

Little by little the bird makes his nest.

A tiny knife is better than your nail.

All that you do not know is greater than you.

Only the knife knows what is in the heart of the yam.

The cat knows and the rat knows that the barrel of maize will remain intact.

Flattery is more dangerous than a two-edged knife.

It is not with its ordinary walk that a cat catches a rat.

The spark says he is mad, but he will never take the road to the river.

The dead do not know the price of sheets.

You cannot sleep on a mat and then speak evil of it.

A little dog is very brave in front of his master's house.

The little fellow does what he can, the big fellow what he wants.

The old pot cooks good food.

Every day the wooden spoon goes to the home of the wooden trough, but one day it will be the turn of the wooden trough to go to the house of the wooden spoon.

I have come to milk the cow and not to count the calves.

Run from the rain, fall into the river.

Every donkey brays in his own pasture.

You must sleep with John to know how he snores.

The wild pig knows on what tree to scratch himself.

He who advises you to buy a greedy horse in the rainy season does not help you feed him in the dry season.

The stick that beats the white dog will beat the black dog too.

Don't leave the donkey in order to beat the packsaddle.

All kinds of timber are wood, but mapou is not mahogany.

When a cockroach gives a dance he never invites a chicken.

When you are very hungry a potato has no peel.

A full stomach says a ripe guava has worms; an empty stomach says, Let me see.

The goat's business is none of the sheep's affair.

You know how to run but you don't know how to hide.

When the cat's stomach is full it says that rats are bitter.

He who strikes the blow forgets, he who bears the marks remembers.

If you had not been looking at the sky you would not have seen it was overcast.

Do not lose a whole ovenful for the sake of one loaf.

Each firefly lights the pathway for his own eyes.

A comrade's house is not a public market.

What God has laid up for you the flood will not carry away.

By-Products of the Good News

T he dinner table had no extra leaves extending it for guests tonight. Tomorrow David would be on the same flight to Miami with me, on his return to school.

Wallace served the chicken with rice and gravy. There were yams, green peas, turnips, and molded carrot salad.

Whenever Wallace returns to the States, he lectures widely to church groups about the problems of Haiti.

Not all of Haiti's problems can be blamed on lack of sanitation, hurricanes and overpopulation. Saving them from parasitic diseases and from death by starvation—one claims no priority over the other—"we help them only by showing them how to help themselves," he insists. He questions the limited permanent good accomplished in pouring billions from the U.S. treasury in foreign giveaway aid—Haiti can profit most from help in land reclamation, education, and industrial development. Like other undeveloped countries, Haiti cannot afford graft. When money is assigned, it is rare that the entire sum reaches its destination. Underlings help themselves as the appropriation moves along, like squirrels filching corn from an open crib. Only when the whole moral standard rises will that stop.

The Haitian farmer has progressed from food gathering to food growing, and now he must take the next step to conservation, or tomorrow will be too late to save this still-lovely land.

"Perhaps you know," Eleanor was saying, "the Haitian government decorated Wallace in 1958, gave him the Cross of Honor and Merit, and made him a knight of the order. After the hurricanes he was presented the Red Cross, their decoration for distinguished service, and later was knighted with the Chevalier Award which cited his work program philosophy of teaching the people. He also influenced the U.S. government in its worldwide program, 'Work for Food'."

The Voodoo drums beat irrepressibly across the night. Those around the table waited for Wallace to continue:

The mission's outlet shop is small but its potential promises to boost the economic plight of the immediate area from want to hopeful existence.

The agricultural experiment center, small though tested, is convincing rural farm families to take not only cabbages and carrots to market, but spinach, cellery, cauliflower, broccoli, asparagus, sweet peppers, peaches, and strawberries, for they see a startling pickup in the money they bring home. Already strawberries bring one dollar a pound. It takes only sixteen berries to make a pound of the kind we had for breakfast this morning.

Frank Bishop, professor of botany from Goshen College, comes down two or three times a year to help us with experiments in propagating the most successful varieties for Haitian soil and climate. The Mennonites are strong on service. Their work on the island is evident in upgrading chicken raising as well as farm produce. Obviously, strains that come from regions similar are more dependable. But where rain hastens the conversion of limestone to productive soil, fog and moisture— the constant humidity ranges twenty to forty percent and rises to one hundred percent every night—encourage fungus diseases, stem and root rot. The California varieties of broccoli, strawberries, celery, tomatoes and potatoes are most successful. Again, some insects, like yellow butterflies, ravage the cabbages and beets in swarms so dense, they smear the windshield and coat the radiator. Another boon, humus compost reduces the need for rotation.

Then, water, the very foundation of life and, like the soil, subject to abuse and misuse is both blessing and bane. Careful management of existing water resources, with conservation during rainy seasons to sustain the people during dry seasons is this thirsty island's equally critical problem.

Of the three distinct mountain ranges in the central region, separated by valleys, the most important river is the Artibonite, two hundred miles long, which drains a three hundred square mile area. Peligre Lake, nine square miles in area was created from the river as a part of the 1969 irrigation project. The dam provides electric power. When the turbines are kept running, that is. Destitute villagers are credited with devising as many as fifty two ways, some methods unknown to electrical science, of tapping the lines for an astounding reduction in power.

Deforestation influences the economy of the river basin. The mountain slopes, denuded of standing timber, are eroded by flash floods that send unchecked torrents down upon the plains to gully the earth, to loosen and carry great slices from the heights, and to shear away sections of road below. In one rainstorm a curve may be reduced to a scant camion width along a steep precipice that drops a fast mile to the wild river gorge below. In the rainy season even the best roads may be too dangerous to travel.

Large scale effort in the schools to instill conservation may be rear-guard effort, but it can be saving. Now, only the new thinking Haitian Christian is convinced of his responsibility to nature, that he is a temporary tenant, answerable to his descendants. For these measures to work in time only funds can help. Plus some degree of enforcement to stem the wanton exploitation until the Haitian can see that he is destroying his future. Government is showing interest in our terracing practices. The past two years Wally has amazed us all with his reforestation successes. An agency of the United Nations took note and began working with the Haitian Department of Agriculture convinced that Wally's methods are right.

"Wally, has turned second generation Burbank," confirmed Eleanor. "His childhood shared Granny's gardening bent, his growing up years at his father's side experimenting with agriculture and animal husbandry provided the backup for experimental know-how. His studies of the soil, the temperatures, and the rainfall are scientifically dependable. He is proving that our denuded mountainsides will sustain certain rapidly growing pines and oaks for firewood. Some black cherry, basswood, and chestnut oak will grow along with the native hardwoods for lumber and cabinet woods. And, to Granny's insistent delight, his year-old seedling rootstocks whip-grafted with peach and apple scions in 1977 produced sweet fruit in 1978!"

"The secret," added Wally, "is to dig a waist-deep hole in the limestone shelf, fill it with earth and compost. The curious come from all over the island, observe his techniques of propagation and grafting and, no longer indifferent, take home starters."

Wally's trial and effort nurseries produced 250,000 seedlings in 1977 now set out and growing. In 1978 his seedlings numbered a million.

Life giving peripherals are all of these—high lysine corn, fancy fruits, bon vivant vegetables, better animals, terraces, schools and churches—by-products of the Good News. Even nonbelievers and skeptics see. But without the transformation of which Jesus spoke to Nicodemus, old ways don't change. Wallace and Eleanor and Granny were all saying what Eleanor was putting into words: "The love of Christ constraineth us... to pioneer, cut jeep trails in the brush country of the northwest, go on farther on foot; to reach the remote coast al areas by sailboat... and now to nurture the new life in little churches and schools all over the island... these are the products of the call and compulsion which brought us to Haiti and now keep us here."

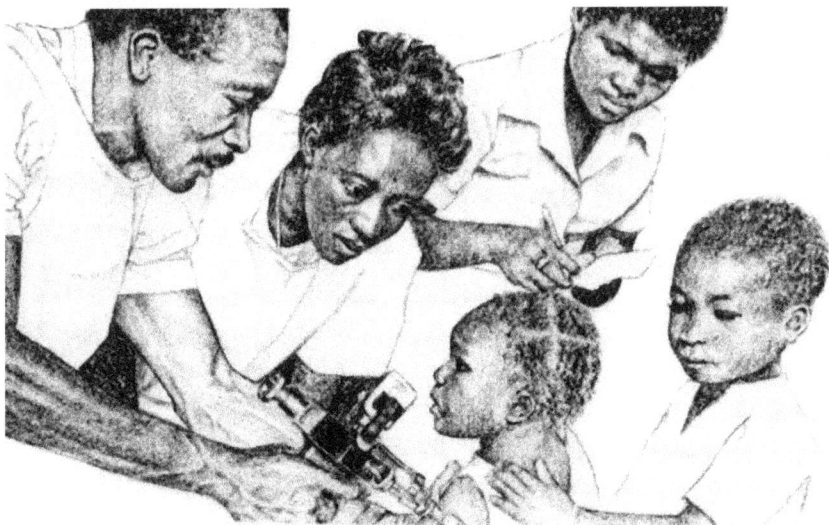

A far cry from Granny's simple dispensary under the avocado trees, the mission hospital now ministers to thousands.

Epilogue

Deserted now, the high mountain road, innocent in the moonlight, had become a silver-white ribbon in a whole soft night turned luminescent silver.

David, striding along with me on our last hike up the mountain, betrayed perhaps more than any other a deeper love for this land in which he had grown up as a missionary kid.

"So many stars. We're nearer the equator. There must be millions more visible from here..."

"No city lights to compete. We see them in the glory and wonder that Job did... and David... and the shepherds on the Judean hillsides."

God's universe stretched into an infinity of overwhelming splendor. Amid myriads of stars we could define some of the constellations—meandering Eridanus, Taurus, Orion, and Lepus, and the distant clustered Pleiades—in a glittering canopy streaked with the Milky Way. Under the spell of this sublime expanse, if one could have and hold one brief moment of uplift and transport, it might be on that lonely high road, braced by the clean mountain air and the steady uphill hike.

We stopped to lean on a low stone wall.

The silence was broken by the distant beep of a French car, then we heard the plaintive throb of the Voodoo drums.

The road uncoiled above us like a spring released by the studded radiance overhead, wound around us and across the valley to a steady glow of earthly reality at the other end— the mission Christmas star.

Profiles

WALLACE TURNBULL—mission Director and co-founder of the Fermathe mission compound and one hundred thirty-nine outpost churches on the island. Also son-in-law of Granny Holdeman.

ELEANOR—Granny's missionary daughter who came to Haiti to visit her mother and returned the following year to marry Wallace, with whom she has shared the trials and joys of more than thirty years in the work.

WALLY, WALTER, DAVID—the three Turnbull sons. Wally and his wife, Betty Brune manage the self-help program, reforestation, agricultural development, and the rural education ministry of the mission. Walter (Sandy) directs the advanced education program and his wife Mary Henk runs the child sponsorship ministry. David was trained in diesel mechanics in Nebraska and in St. Paul, Minnesota before returning to help at the mission.

ZENAS AND NEVART—retired missionaries, affectionately known by all as Uncle Zenas and Aunt Nevart.

Glossary

abobo—amen

asson—a gourd rattle

Badagri—(bebe) the small Voodoo drum; segon is the middle one; (maman) assorter, the large one. The drum is the soul of the dance. A sacred instrument, it is the receptacle of a loa; is saluted, given food, dressed and put to sleep. Tambou travaille is the common or work drum, a sort of rural telegraph, transmitting messages with uncanny speed

bocor—witch doctor, almost same as houngan, the Voodoo priest

camion—a large open bus with hard wooden benches set on a truck chassis. These brilliantly painted and quaintly named conveyances chug and lumber gaily over all Haiti's public roads, solidly packed with people and their household goods, vegetables, and everything from baskets to bongo drums roped to the top

camionette—pickup or station wagon, a smaller conveyance than the camion

carrefour—a crossroads of special significance in Voodoo rites

kombit—get together work bee, as for spring planting

cours de famille—a family compound, corresponding to a village.

Creole(Kreyòl)—spoken by every Haitian, but the educated speak French and often Spanish as well. This language of the masses is not a corruption of French but rather Old Norman French such as was spoken by the colonials of the 1600's and now injected with some modern French, with a few English, Spanish, Indian, and some African words. The syntax is English

dances—banda, congo, petro, nago are sacred dances; merengue, limbo, coupe are common dances; Calypso and merengue are dissimilar only in that one melody is English, the other French

hounfor—inner sanctum, Voodoo temple, altar, shrine

houngan—Voodoo priest (wizard, magician, witch doctor)

hounsi bossale and housi kanzo—assist houngan as choir and dancers language—spirit talk (old African) in a Voodoo service

loa—Congo word for spirit, deity

mambo—Voodoo priestess; also Voodoo dance popular in U.S.

peristyle—meeting place for Voodoo ritual usually an arbor with a center pole

possession—culminating moment in a sacred dance, when one of the faithful is mounted by a loa, descends into his body, speaks and acts through him in compulsive, frantic dancing or writhing seizure. The possessed, ridden by the loa, hyperventilates, breaks out in sweat, wears an anguished expression, goes into spasmodic convulsions

Rada—family of patron dieties

Rara—festival that occurs before Easter

vèvè—Voodoo ritual drawing, very artistic, usually with cornmeal (also, vever)

Voodoo—possibly from African Dahomey dialect word vodi, meaning worship; feared by the French colonists who saw it as a mysterious and powerful cohesive among the slaves; vaudau

zombie—exhumed or resuscitated being in whom a living death has been produced during a drug produced cataleptic trance. The revived victim is thereafter mindless, but able to perform physical slave labor. The Haitian Criminal Code forbids use of these drugs.

About the Author

This is the author's first sounder, if one counts producing a book under cover as Mildred Anderson's one journalistic achievement after spending most of her life in the field.

Along with her doctor-husband-editor, Wick, Mildred helped publish a medical journal, a weekly newspaper, and many other periodicals over more than three decades. When asked why she never wrote a book, she twits, "We were too busy producing a first edition to write about it."

Looking back over those busy years of life in a small Mississippi town with her husband whose practice was mostly rural, and who helped run his town almost as a one-man chamber of commerce (yet who was listed in Who's Who in America 1937-1969), she recalls, "I was twirling in half a dozen roles. One needs leisure to write. My day and I were indeed overspent if I had kept the presses running, helped Wick prevent or promote certain civic happenings, depended on Koot to add the right amount of water to extend the soup for two unexpected legislators who stayed for lunch, answered the phone all hours, and touched base with daughters Jane and Nancy.

"Now, with life less strenuous, to have the privilege of writing about my long-time friend, this wonderfully heroic woman who has spent thirty-odd years of her mature life swabbing the sores and showing The Way in perhaps the darkest corner of our hemisphere, has been an excursion of joy.

"And may you, dear reader, find a day with Granny Holdeman and the Turnbulls enrichingly delightsome... and perhaps one happy day even find yourself sharing the heartbeat and an unforgettable evening with the other guests and celebrities around Eleanor's table at the mission at Fermathe.